Voices from the Plain of Jars

this new edition supported by
Figure Foundation

Voices from the Plain of Jars

Life under an Air War

Second edition

Edited by FRED BRANFMAN
with essays and drawings by LAOTIAN VILLAGERS

THE UNIVERSITY OF WISCONSIN PRESS

The University of Wisconsin Press
1930 Monroe Street, 3rd Floor
Madison, Wisconsin 53711-2059
uwpress.wisc.edu

3 Henrietta Street
London WC2E 8LU, England
eurospanbookstore.com

Library of Congress Cataloging-in-Publication Data

Branfman, Fred.
Voices from the Plain of Jars : life under an air war / compiled, with
an introduction and epilogue, by Fred Branfman. — 2nd ed.
p. cm. — (New perspectives in Southeast Asian studies)
Previous ed.: New York : Harper & Row, 1972.
Includes bibliographical references.
ISBN 978-0-299-29224-9 (pbk. : alk. paper) — ISBN 978-0-299-29223-2 (e-book)
1. Vietnam War, 1961–1975—Aerial operations, American.
2. Vietnam War, 1961–1975—Laos—Jars, Plain of. 3. Jars, Plain of (Laos)
I. Title. II. Series: New perspectives in Southeast Asian studies.
DS557.A65B67 2013
959.704´33594—dc23
2012032677

In memory of

SAO DOUMMA,

a twenty-five-year-old woman from the Plain of Jars,
killed in a bombing raid in August 1969,
and all the others

Contents

Foreword

Reflections on History's Largest Air War

ALFRED W. MCCOY

Though this volume seems, at first glance, a slender collection of short statements and simple sketches, it is arguably the most important single book to emerge from the Vietnam War. Originally published more than forty years ago, *Voices from the Plain of Jars* is a collective memoir of the secret air war over neutral Laos, written, in part, by the ordinary Lao peasants who suffered under its bombs. Since there is no other book written by the villagers of Indochina, these "voices" can, in a sense, speak for the countless Vietnamese and Cambodians who also suffered under the U.S. bombing. Not only does the 2.1 million tons of bombs dropped on Laos from 1965 to 1973 rank among the largest air wars of the twentieth century, exceeded only by the 2.7 million tons dropped on Cambodia, but it also was a precursor for the way wars would be fought in the twenty-first century and beyond.[1] Through a unique fusion of first-person accounts and policy analysis by its author, Fred Branfman, this book recovers an obscure yet significant moment in military history and documents an air war so intense that it became a testing ground for a new form of global force projection.

This secret air war was part of a clandestine intervention in Laos necessitated by a major strategic miscalculation. As part of its larger Cold War foreign policy of containing communism behind its own iron curtain, Washington formed a strategic alliance with Laos in the mid-1950s, specifically with its right-wing faction, marked by overt military aid and covert CIA

---

1. Channapha Khamvongsa and Elaine Russell, "Legacies of War: Cluster Bombs in Laos," *Critical Asian Studies* 41, no. 2 (2001): 281; Taylor Owen and Ben Kiernan, "Bombs Over Cambodia," *The Walrus* (October 2006), http://walrusmagazine.com/author/taylor-owen-and-ben-kiernan, accessed March 20, 2013.

political manipulations. During its first five years inside Laos, the agency maneuvered to keep both communists and neutralists out of power, using blatant bribes and electoral manipulations in what first seemed to many American officials an amusingly backward nation. According to a classified CIA history, Director Allen Dulles styled his agency's attempts at blocking a neutralist coalition in 1958 as a "youthful prank"; in follow-up elections, the agency, with this same puckish spirit, colluded in assigning the communist Pathet Lao 1,927 votes since that was the year CIA agent Stuart Methven was born; and field operatives backed General Phoumi Nosavan in a bungled bid to become the country's right-wing dictator.[2]

By 1960, such crude, capricious intervention had sparked a strongly nationalist reaction and brought Soviet air transports to Vientiane loaded with military aid for the neutralist faction, plunging the country into a civil war so volatile that it required resolution by an international conference at Geneva in 1962. Under the terms of that agreement, the Kennedy administration agreed to the diplomatic neutralization of Laos and reduced its formal military presence. Within just three years, however, this entente proved a major strategic miscalculation when North Vietnamese troops began infiltrating through southern Laos, threatening Washington's strategy for winning the Vietnam War. Barred from conventional military operations by the Geneva agreement, the White House opted for covert intervention, with secret Air Force bombing in southern Laos and CIA paramilitary operations in the north.[3]

As part of this clandestine intervention, the Kennedy administration launched a massive secret war in northern Laos, which Ambassador William Sullivan called "the other war," meaning it was somehow separate from the air war in the south. In this covert operation, U.S. military—apart from trying to slow the advance of Pathet Lao guerrillas—built a major radar base on Phou Pha Thi mountain for guiding fighters on bombing missions against North Vietnam and established a network of hilltop militia bases so that Hmong tribesmen and Thai mercenaries could conduct local combat operations and launch covert forays into North Vietnam.

2. Thomas L. Ahern Jr., *Undercover Armies: CIA and Surrogate Warfare in Laos, 1961–1973* (Washington, DC: Center for the Study of Intelligence, Central Intelligence Agency, 2006), 11–12.

3. Victor B. Anthony and Richard R. Sexton, *The United States Air Force in Southeast Asia: The War in Northern Laos, 1954–1973* (Washington, DC: Center for Air Force History, United States Air Force, 1993), 71–73, 107–33.

From 1965 to 1973, tiny, landlocked Laos, then rated as the world's poorest nation, thus became the site of history's largest air war. From a few dozen missions daily in 1965, U.S. Air Force operations escalated steadily to reach a peak of 200 combat sorties daily over Laos between 1968 and 1970.[4] Even as the United States withdrew its ground forces from Vietnam after 1969, the Air Force bombardment of Laos continued and, in certain areas, intensified. Under the pressures of the general withdrawal from Vietnam, total air sorties for Indochina dropped from a peak of 20,000 per month in 1969 to 10,000 by 1971, and aircraft in theater declined from 1,800 to 1,100. But, reflecting the strategic significance of Laos within the wider Vietnam War, the Air Force shifted its residual capacity to focus overwhelmingly on this tiny country. From its four main bases just across the Mekong River in Thailand, the Air Force maintained, even in mid-1971, a fleet of 330 aircraft, including 125 of its workhorse F-4 fighter-bombers.[5] Additional fighter aircraft from aircraft carriers off the coast and bases in South Vietnam, as well as B-52s based in Guam and Thailand, were also deployed against Laos. Even as the Nixon administration withdrew ground troops from South Vietnam, it tripled the bombing of Laos, from an annual average of 129,482 tons in 1965–68 to an average of 387,466 tons per year in 1969–72.

Inside Laos, air activity was divided into two main arenas. Operation "Barrel Roll" provided tactical air support for CIA paramilitary operations against Lao guerrillas in the north and strategic bombing to destroy the supporting civilian infrastructure. Operation "Steel Tiger" deployed electronic sensors and massive bombardment in an attempt to cut North Vietnamese infiltration along the Ho Chi Minh Trail in the south. Reflecting U.S. strategic priorities, Steel Tiger in the south received about 85 percent of all sorties flown over Indochina circa 1970, while Barrel Roll in the north, the main focus of this book, received about 15 percent.[6]

As well as tripling in tonnage after 1968, the aircraft and ordnance for Barrel Roll's bombardment of northern Laos grew more lethal. Most importantly, the tonnage dropped by B-52 bombers on the north increased

4. Ibid., 333.

5. Air Force, Headquarters, Pacific Air Forces, "Corona Harvest: USAF Force Withdrawal from Southeast Asia, 1 January 1970–30 June 1971 (U)," May 31, 1972, pp. 53–54, 76, 78, accessed June 5, 2012, http://www.scribd.com/doc/51912794/USAF-Withdrawal-from-Southeast-Asia-1-JANUARY-1970-30-JUNE-1971.

6. Anthony and Sexton, *United States Air Force in Southeast Asia*, 333.

from 4,200 tons in 1970 to 25,000 tons in 1972.[7] To improve the accuracy of fast-flying jets like the Phantom F-4 that cruised at 600 miles per hour, the Air Force deployed the Snake Eye high-drag bomb equipped with flaps, thereby doubling its accuracy. By photo mapping the entire Plain of Jars, the main air base in nearby Udorn, Thailand, produced a photographic grid with coordinates for every feature, allowing transmission of target coordinates directly into the bombing computers of F-4 fighters for deadly accuracy.[8]

But, above all, the Air Force introduced a more efficient cluster bomb unit (CBU). At the bombing's start in 1965, U.S. aircraft had relied on the Rockeye II (Cluster Bomb Mark 20), a seven-foot-long clamshell with fins that opened, midflight, to release "247 shaped-charge bomblets," each one detonating upon impact to discharge 200 steel pellets and thereby blasting an area the size of a football field with nearly 50,000 pellets. After 1970, U.S. fighter jets carried the CBU-38, with a reusable canister containing 40 fourteen-pound, antipersonnel bomblets with "bigger fragments, greater fragment velocity, and more incendiary effect." In a two-second bomb run, each F-4 Phantom fighter could disperse its normal load of three canisters to cover a 200 by 600 foot area with 120 bomblets. Instead of striking directly at enemy forces, the Air Force used this new ordnance to destroy "the enemy logistic network," allowing a wider, less discriminate bombing in civilian areas.[9]

By April 1973, the Air Force had dropped an estimated 2.1 million tons of bombs on Laos, which was equivalent to the entire tonnage the United States dropped on industrialized Germany and Japan during the whole of World War II. Of this total, about 1.7 million tons were concentrated in a strategic bombing of the Ho Chi Minh Trail infiltration route through a narrow, lightly populated mountain corridor in southern Laos, producing limited collateral damage. But some 321,000 tons, twice the bombardment

---

7. U.S. Congress, *Congressional Record—Senate: May 14, 1975* (Washington, DC: Government Printing Office, 1975), 14266.

8. Anthony and Sexton, *United States Air Force in Southeast Asia*, 336.

9. Ibid.; "Rockeye II Mark 20," US Naval Museum of Armament and Technology, China Lake, California, accessed June 8, 2012, http://www.chinalakemuseum.org/exhibits/rockeye.shtml; entries for "CBU-2/A: 360 'BLU-3/B Pineapple'" and "CBU-46B/A: 640 'BLU-66/B Pineapple'" from Greg Goebel, *Vectors*, "[2.0] Dumb Bombs (2): Cluster Munitions and Other Bombs," accessed June 8, 2012, http://www.vectorsite.net/twbomb_02.html.

of Japan during World War II, were dropped on the Plain of Jars region in northeastern Laos, a populated area with some 200,000 people and the site of the ancient Lao Pheun civilization.[10] During the years of peak bombing on the Plain of Jars, its peasant population suffered heavy loss of life and property. Many were reduced to living in caves and working their fields in the few hours of twilight between the daylight tactical bombing and the nighttime strafing by AC-47 "Spooky" gunships.[11] Farmers who ventured into their fields during daylight faced sudden death from the air, a reality captured in this book's sketches of burning houses and dismembered bodies.

Apart from the heavy loss of life, this aerial bombardment also covered portions of northern Laos with countless thousands of antipersonnel bomblets that, even today, some forty years later, continue to maim and kill hundreds of residents every year in the Plain of Jars area. Since Congress approved the USAID's Leahy War Victims Fund in 1993, the United States has provided $51 million to assist in the removal of unexplored ordnance (UXO) in Laos, including a special appropriation of $5.1 million in 2010. This sum, however, has done relatively little to address the problem of the millions of unexploded cluster bomblets left behind by this U.S. aerial bombardment. Since the war ended in 1974, approximately 20,000 civilians have been killed or maimed by these unexploded bombs, and the number continues to mount. Only 0.28 percent of the area contaminated by UXOs has been cleared as of 2012, and countless subsistence-level farmers are still denied use of the land they need to survive.[12]

However, this bombing campaign is much more than an historical footnote to the Vietnam War. Under the pressures of history's longest and largest air war, the Air Force experimented with technological innovations, including computer-directed bombing, new antipersonnel bombs, aerial gunships of unprecedented power, and drone warfare. As the official Air Force history of this campaign explains, established military doctrine stated that "air power could not gain, hold, or occupy terrain; only ground forces could." But, with the Geneva agreement blocking intervention and the Royal Lao Army demoralized by a devastating defeat in 1969 that "virtually erased these

10. U.S. Congress, *Congressional Record—Senate: May 14, 1975*, 14266.

11. Anthony and Sexton, *United States Air Force in Southeast Asia*, 296–97.

12. "The Unexploded Ordnance (UXO) Problem and Operational Progress in the Lao PDR—Official Figures," from the National Regulatory Authority for UXO/Mine Action in the Lao PDR, November 2010.

forces as a factor in the war," "air power was all the [U.S.] embassy or the
Royal Laotian Government had."[13] When President Nixon finally admitted
the existence of this air war in March 1970 after six years of secret operations, he could, moreover, defend U.S. observance of Laos's neutrality by
saying, "The United States has no ground forces in Laos."[14] Through this
conjuncture of international and local factors, Washington was forced to rely
on airpower in ways that demanded innovation.

By the time this bombing campaign drew to a close in 1973, the Air Force
had overturned one of modern warfare's fundamental axioms by showing,
for the first time, that airpower alone had the capacity to take hold of terrain
without any infantry on the ground. Achieving this tactical breakthrough
required a massive bombardment of unequalled intensity that was delivered
without concern for collateral damage visited on the ordinary villagers below.
Indeed, in the forty-some years since the bombing of Laos ended, the U.S.
military has relied on air power as its main strike force in Bosnia, Kosovo,
Kurdistan, Afghanistan, and Libya. Looking forward, Washington's future
operations overseas are likely to rely primarily, perhaps even solely, upon
airpower, making this long-forgotten air war over Laos the progenitor for
warfare in the twenty-first century. In short, the bombing of Laos is a small
topic of enormous import for an understanding of global power projection,
both past and future.

In marked contrast to the hundreds of journalists who filled the rows
of folding chairs for daily military briefings at the Joint Public Affairs Office
(JUSPAO) in downtown Saigon, just a handful of freelance reporters hung
about Vientiane, trying to ferret out a few scraps of information from covert
operatives whose diplomatic cover helped conceal an elaborate, secret warfare
apparatus. For nearly six years, the massive bombing campaign saturated the
mountains of Laos, yet the operation somehow remained hidden from the
American press and public. Even when Congress finally exposed the operation in 1970, reporters found it an impossible war to cover because there was
no accessible data about its structure, scale, or impact. In sum, history's
largest air war was effectively conducted within an information blackout.

Serving in Laos as an educational adviser, Fred Branfman was the only
observer who discovered the full scale of the air war and documented its

---

13. Anthony and Sexton, *United States Air Force in Southeast Asia*, 106, 239.
14. Ibid., 327.

impact upon civilian refugees who had fled from the Plain of Jars region. By conducting extensive interviews with the Lao refugees from the bombing, pilots and personnel at bases in Thailand and South Vietnam, and a captain in charge of target selection at the U.S. embassy in Vientiane, Branfman became the first to document the sheer scale of the massive air war over Laos. Most importantly, he was able to draw upon his prior experience in the villages as he made contact with refugees from the bombed areas of northern Laos and learned about the impact that the air war had had upon their lives. Instead of interviewing these villagers and serving as their surrogate voice, Branfman asked these peasant farmers to write first-person accounts of the bombing raids and illustrate them with their own detailed drawings of temples, houses, farmhouses, and fields being destroyed by detonation. Among the thousands of books on the Vietnam War, this is the only one written by ordinary villagers, whose voices give us not only a sense of the suffering on the Plain of Jars but also an understanding of the impact upon civilians across Indochina who lived under the 6.7 million tons of bombs that were dropped on the region.

The result is an extraordinary work that is both immediate and timeless. At the time *Voices from the Plain of Jars* was published back in 1972, the undeniable integrity of the eyewitness testimonies and the powerful visual evidence of the drawings shattered the six-year silence that had shrouded the secret bombing of Laos and contributed to a congressional ban on air activity over Cambodia.

Today, some forty years after the book's first publication, the significance of its message has, if anything, increased. For even as Branfman immersed himself in the suffering of the Lao peasants, he understood that he was not only witnessing the present but seeing the future. In articles, lectures, and congressional testimony, he argued that the air war over Laos had forged the future strategy for U.S. global force projection. He predicted, with uncommon prescience, that American soldiers would no longer fight and die on the ground as they had in Vietnam, but Washington would, in future wars, engage in automated warfare, using airpower to take and hold ground by sheer force of aerial bombardment.

Laos served as a testing ground for forging this new global strategy and thus offers the rest of the world an eloquent but cautionary message about U.S. foreign policy, today and in the future. That message, Branfman establishes, is that such bombing is deeply traumatic for societies subjected to

it. While the secret air war over Laos devastated the Plain of Jars, its inhabitants suffered in silence, leaving only these drawing as as a visual record
of the destruction. But today even those in the most remote villages can
communicate their suffering to a wider world through cell phones, wireless
Internet, or citizen journalists equipped with digital cameras and texting
technology.

More changes are in store as world tensions persist and technology continues its relentless progress. After a decade of aerial warfare over Afghan-
Pakistan borderlands, collateral damage from conventional bombing and
unmanned aerial vehicles called "drones" has already roiled relations with
the Karzai government in Kabul and aroused strong, popular opposition in
neighboring Pakistan.[15] While the technological trajectory toward a capacity
for worldwide aerial force projection is accelerating, the potential political
opposition from communities using elements of the same communications
technology is also a possibility, complicating Washington's bid for continuing global dominion via aerospace alone. While the form of this automated
aerial warfare and possible diplomatic agreements that might restrain its
use are still very much in flux, Branfman's slender volume stands as telling
reminder for the devastating impact this realpolitik exercise of global power
can have for the ordinary villagers worldwide who might suffer its collateral
damage.

15. See Declan Walsh, Eric Schmitt, and Ihsanullah Tipu Mehsud, "Drones at Issue
as US Rebuilds Ties to Pakistan," *New York Times*, March 18, 2012.

Textual Note

These essays and drawings were prepared by Laotian survivors of the bombing and destruction of the Plain of Jars. Bouangeun Luangpraseuth and I then collected the material in a half-dozen refugee camps in the Vientiane Plain between September and December 1970.

Four major obstacles affected the securing of these documents. The first was language. Few Westerners cared to learn Laotian and because of that were almost completely cut off from the peasants. Had we not known Laotian, the project would have been doomed from the start.

The second barrier was political. Because most of the refugees had fled one form or another of American firepower, they tended to distrust, fear, or hate Americans and were either quite reticent or transparently insincere around Americans—at first. Basically, though, Laotians were among the most open, tolerant, and warm people anywhere. As we continued visiting the camps and talking with the same people again and again, the barriers slowly began to come down with people opening up to us. In the end, though, the key factor was that the refugees trusted my close friend Bouangeun, whom I called "Ngeun." It was he who collected the drawings and essays at some risk to himself, as he had to hide them in his shirt when passing through police checkpoints between the refugee camps and downtown Vientiane city.

The third problem was military. Refugees ran great physical risk in telling outsiders things contrary to the American-supported line, and ran an even greater risk committing such thoughts to paper. Those too talkative were liable to be accused of being "Communists," and thereby detained, arrested, mistreated, or worse. In our case, however, we were fortunate enough to befriend several refugees trusted by their fellows who were willing to take the risk of collecting these essays. They did so with the understanding that we would not take down the names of the authors; nor did we wish to know their identities.

The fourth problem, and the most important one, was cultural. Westerners had been conditioned to see the village people of Indochina as semiliterate, dull, and unimaginative peasants. I shared some of this cultural conditioning. Although I had lived among Laotian peasants for several years and had talked with the Plain of Jars refugees for countless hours from September 1969 on, it at first simply did not occur to me to collect these essays from them until a year later. It was in September 1970 that a thought occurred to me. I said to Ngeun one day, "It's a pity these people cannot read or write, I bet they would have significant stories to tell." Ngeun responded "Hwai! They can read and write better than you can." Shocked, I asked him if he thought he could collect stories from them about their lives under the air war. He said he could. He did. And this book is the result.

Given these circumstances, we feel that these essays and drawings present as moving and accurate a picture of what the war was like for the peasants of Indochina as is soon likely to emerge. Frankly, we ourselves have been amazed at the emotion, style, and experience that were transmitted so well despite language barriers. We suggested that they might discuss such topics as the economy, education, and farming, but focus on the impact of the 1964–69 bombing on their lives.

In addition, we encountered problems translating words for concepts that did not have English equivalents or translating expressions that did not exist outside of Laotian peasant life. Fortunately, I was helped by a gifted Lao translator, Hiem Phommachanh, and we opted for factual, literal translations as close in meaning to the original as possible. The only exceptions to this were the poetic essays from the traditional Lao singer and the poet. Since much of Laotian culture is transmitted orally from father to son, each village selects particular individuals to be specially trained in that oral tradition. These traditional singers sing at weddings, funerals, and religious occasions, often composing poems about current events and delivering them in the traditional mode. Obviously, such poems do not lend themselves to literal translation, and so these pieces have been translated rather freely.

These then are the voices from the Plain of Jars. The people themselves say that they come from "Xieng Khouang," which is the name of the province in which the Plain is found. At times, however, they may also refer to the town of Xieng Khouang, which is the capital of the province. Each province is divided into districts (*muongs*), subdistricts or cantons (*tassengs*), and hamlets (*bans*).

When reading these essays, the reader is cautioned against drawing conclusions about the writers' political sympathies. In an effort to encourage the Laotians to write as freely as possible, we specifically asked them not to state which side they preferred or to engage in polemics either for or against the Royal Lao Government or the Pathet Lao.

Perhaps some readers may be moved to dismiss what is written here and to ascribe the words to "exaggeration" or even "propaganda." We, the translators, cannot vouch for the truth of each and every incident recorded here, but we do know that (a) American officials have admitted bombing the Plain for five and a half years, from May 1964 to September 1969; (b) on the basis of available figures, at least twenty-five thousand sorties were flown against the Plain and seventy-five thousand tons of ordnance were dropped on it; and (c) an official United States Information Service survey accepted testimony from refugees that 95 percent of them had had their villages bombed, that nearly two-thirds of them had seen someone killed or injured by the bombs, and that in 80 percent of such cases, the victim was a villager and not a soldier.[1] Much research since the end of the bombing in 1973, including village by village surveys conducted by the Lao PDJ National Regulatory Authority, has confirmed what the villagers describe here.[2]

There is thus no reason whatsoever to believe that the people who wrote these essays and drew these pictures exaggerated in any way what happened to them.

---

1. U.S. Congress, Senate, Committee on the Judiciary, *War-Related Civilian Problems in Indochina: Part II: Laos and Cambodia* (April 21 and 22, 1971), in *Hearings before the Subcommittee to Investigate Problems Connected with Refugees and Escapees*, 92d Cong., 1st sess. (Washington, DC: Government Printing Office, 1970).

2. "The Unexploded Ordnance (UXO) Problem and Operational Progress in the Lao PDR—Official Figures," from the National Regulatory Authority for UXO/Mine Action in the Lao PDR, November 2010.

Introduction

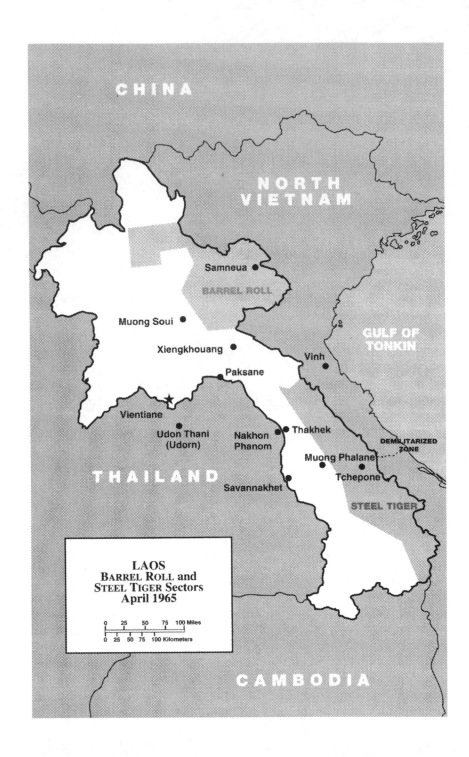

CHINA

NORTH VIETNAM

Samneua

BARREL ROLL

GULF OF TONKIN

Muong Soui

Xiengkhouang

Vinh

Paksane

Vientiane

Udon Thani (Udorn)

Nakhon Phanom

Thakhek

DEMILITARIZED ZONE

Muong Phalane

Tchepone

THAILAND

Savannakhet

STEEL TIGER

LAOS
BARREL ROLL and
STEEL TIGER Sectors
April 1965

0   25   50   75   100 Miles
0   25   50   75   100 Kilometers

CAMBODIA

Laos and the Advent
of Automated War

In September 1969, after a recorded history of seven hundred years, the Plain of Jars disappeared.

The Plain, located in northeastern Laos, was destroyed by a bombing campaign that marked one of the most significant events of the twentieth century: the advent of unilateral and secret U.S. Executive Branch automated warfare. Laos was the first occasion in which the majority of fighting was done by aircraft, not troops, with the U.S. Air Force dropping 2.1 million tons of bombs on Laos, as much as was dropped on all of Europe and the Pacific theater in World War II. By comparison, fighting on the ground by local troops with guidance from U.S. advisers played a relatively insignificant role.

These 2.1 million tons were part of an overall U.S. bombing campaign that saw a total of 6.7 million tons dropped on Southeast Asia (North and South Vietnam, Cambodia, and Laos). Afterward, only one book emerged that was written by some of the tens of millions of rural Indochinese villagers who lived under the bombs: *Voices from the Plain of Jars*. The authors were the innocents who had made up more than 90 percent of the population and represented those who had suffered the most but were heard from the least. These "voices" are thus the sole record of not only what the people of the Plain of Jars experienced but also of the suffering of millions of others devastated by bombings throughout Indochina, voices that have almost never been heard.

The Plain of Jars—Background

The Plain had been home to a prosperous rural society of some fifty thousand people. Amid mounting conflict in Vietnam, an international agreement signed in 1962 declared neighboring Laos officially neutral. But war continued to rage as the United States continued to use northern Laos as a base from which to attack North Vietnam with a secret army composed of tens of thousands of local tribesmen and mercenaries, forces who were opposed by several thousand North Vietnamese and local Pathet Lao communist troops. After the Pathet Lao occupied the Plain in May 1964, the United States launched a massive air war that leveled village after village. In the next five and a half years, more than seventy-five thousand tons of bombs were dropped on the Plain in more than twenty-five thousand sorties.[1] A simultaneous air campaign targeted the Ho Chi Minh Trail in southern Laos.[2]

American bombers killed and wounded tens of thousands of Laotians. Countless people were buried alive by high explosives, burnt alive by napalm

1. No one knows exactly how many tons of bombs were dropped on the Plain from 1964 to 1969. The Cornell Air War Study, "The Air War in Indochina" (preliminary report, Cornell University. Center for International Studies, October 1971), estimated that approximately 230,000 tons were dropped in northern Laos in 1968 and 1969. (The report has no estimates for the years before 1968.) At the end of the war, official U.S. Air Force figures indicated that the U.S. had dropped 320,000 tons of bombs on northern Laos between 1964 and 1973. (Please see "Indochina War Statistics—Dollars and Deaths," *Congressional Record—Senate: May 14, 1975* [Washington, DC: Government Printing Office, 1975], 14266). Readers interested in learning more about the air war in Laos might be interested in Fred Branfman, "The Era of the Blue Machine," *Washington Monthly*, July 1971; Elaine Russell, "Laos—Living with Unexploded Ordnance: Past Memories and Present Realities," in *Interactions with a Violent Past: Reading Post-Conflict Landscapes in Cambodia, Laos, and Vietnam*, ed. Vatthana Pholsena and Oliver Tappe (Singapore: National University of Singapore, n.d.); and Fred Branfman, "The Laos Automated War Archive," an online archive available upon request from the author at fredbranfman@aol .com. The archive consists of thirty-six pieces on the air war in Laos written between 1969 and 1975. It comprises the most complete description of an air war, from the "top down" and "bottom up," of which we are aware.

2. Most of the pilots bombing northern Laos operated out of Udorn, Korat, and Nakhon Phanom air bases in northeast Thailand. The United States, however, did not allow American reporters to interview pilots at these bases. As late as the fall of 1970, when I visited the Udorn base, aviators were still instructed to deny that they were bombing in northern Laos. To my knowledge, while reporters may have at various times visited these bases, they did not have, and to this day still do not have, the same easy access to American pilots in Thailand that they had, for years, to American pilots in South Vietnam. Much of the bombing was also conducted from bases in South Vietnam, especially Da Nang Air Base, and carriers based in the Gulf of Tonkin.

and white phosphorous, or riddled by antipersonnel bomb pellets. U.S. officials made every effort to conceal these raids, continuing to claim until March 1970 that it was not even bombing in Laos—six months after the Plain had been destroyed—and then continuing to lie by claiming that they had never bombed civilian targets.

The outside world found out about the bombing, however, when CIA advisers decided in September 1969 to force the people of the Plain of Jars to move 230 miles south from their ancestral homes to refugee camps around the capital city of Vientiane, which was controlled by the U.S.-supported Royal Lao Government. As journalists and other Westerners, including myself, began to interview these refugees, they discovered that the people had been secretly bombed for the previous five and a half years.

In several of these refugee camps, survivors from the Plain of Jars wrote the essays and drew the pictures in this book. Here the Plain's inhabitants reveal how aircraft destroyed their homes, storehouses, schools, temples, and bamboo huts built in the forest; how they retreated, first into the forest and then underground, huddling together in tunnels and holes; how rice fields, vegetable gardens, and fruit orchards were rendered barren by the bombs; how water buffalo, cows, chickens, ducks, and pigs were lost to the bombs; and how the bombs killed or wounded their children, parents, grandparents, aunts and uncles, and cousins.

For five and a half years, U.S. Executive Branch officials kept this war secret. When they finally acknowledged the bombing, they denied that civilians had ever been hit. As survivors from the Plain were being herded into refugee camps, former Ambassador William H. Sullivan testified in closed session to the United States Senate that "the Lao, of course, placed restrictions on the strikes that would go into populated areas. The United States Air Force contribution was limited to striking at the logistic routes . . . choke points . . . or at points of concentration which fed into the area where the actual ground battling was taking place. . . . [I]t was the policy not to attack populated areas." His air attaché, Colonel William Tyrrell, was even more explicit: "Villages, even in a free drop zone, would be restricted from bombing."[3]

3. U.S. Congress, Senate, Committee on Foreign Relations, *United States Security Agreements and Commitments Abroad: Kingdom of Laos* (October 21, 1969), in *Hearings before the Subcommittee on United States Security Agreements and Commitments Abroad, United States Senate*, 91st Cong., 1st sess. (Washington, DC: Government Printing Office, 1970), vol. 1, pt. 2, 500, 514.

And when President Nixon first told the American people on March 6, 1970, that the United States had been bombing in Laos for the past six years, he, too, avoided any mention of civilian destruction. "We have continued to conduct air operations," said Nixon. "Our first priority is the Ho Chi Minh Trail. In addition we have continued to carry out reconnaissance flights in northern Laos to fly combat support missions for Laotian forces."[4]

Refugees from the Plain, however, reported that the main victims of the bombing were not military or paramilitary; they were ordinary civilians, particularly older people, mothers, and children who had to remain near their villages to survive. Guerrilla and North Vietnamese soldiers, the putative targets of the attack, traversed the densely carpeted forests of northern Laos relatively unscathed. Subsequent interviews with pilots and others involved in the bombing confirmed the refugees' accounts. The air war targeted mainly villages because they were the only signs of life that could be seen from the air, as I learned during fifteen months of interviewing U.S. Air Force pilots and personnel after I discovered the bombing.

What happened in one location, the Plain of Jars in northern Laos, is the story of this book. The refugees' writings and drawings, however, are also key to understanding the bombing of the rest of Laos that continued until 1973, both in the area north of the Plain of Jars in Houaphanh province and in all of southeastern Laos through which the Ho Chi Minh Trail ran. The destruction of the Plain was only one result of the most massive bombing of civilian targets that had ever occurred.

Was this bombing justified? Making a moral and legal judgment about the bombing of Laos involves two basic questions. First, Did the United States have the right to bomb anywhere in Laos? One's view on America's moral and legal right to bomb at all in Laos depends upon one's overall belief about America's right to intervene militarily in Indochina. Those who believe the United States had a right to wage war in Indochina fundamentally justify the Laos bombing as necessary to winning in South Vietnam. Those who, like the editor, believe that the United States waged an "aggressive war" in Indochina, termed "the supreme international crime" by Chief Justice Robert Jackson at the Nuremberg Trials, see no legal or moral justification

---

4. U.S. Congress, Senate, Committee on the Judiciary, *War-Related Civilian Problems in Indochina: Part II: Laos and Cambodia* (April 21 and 22, 1971), in *Hearings before the Subcommittee to Investigate Problems Connected with Refugees and Escapees*, 92d Cong., 1st sess. (Washington, DC: Government Printing Office, 1970), 43, 45.

whatsoever for leaders dropping a single bomb on Laos.[5] Second, but even if one believes that the United States had the right to bomb in Laos, did the United States have the right to massively bomb civilian targets? The answer to this latter question is unambiguously "no." The bombing of civilians in Laos clearly violated international law, beginning with Article 25 of the 1907 Hague Conventions forbidding the "bombing of undefended towns and villages" and numerous clauses of the UN Charter. U.S. leaders have not tried to defend their bombing of civilian targets. They have simply denied until today that they did so, a tacit admission that the bombing of civilian targets on the Plain of Jars was both immoral and illegal.

More broadly, the Plain of Jars story is key to understanding a new form of warfare, in which machines rather than men did most of the killing. Before Laos, airpower was seen as providing support for ground troops. By the mid-1960s in northeastern Laos, however, the local CIA-supported Hmong and mercenary forces had been decimated. But the CIA continued to draft and force Hmong teenagers to fight, using them as "live bait" to try to draw enemy fire so that aircraft—carrying the brunt of the fighting—would know where to bomb.

Much of the escalation of the bombing of the Plain of Jars was due to bureaucratic infighting between the CIA and Pentagon. The CIA had taken control of U.S. war-making in Laos and sought to demonstrate that its form of clandestine and automated war was more effective than the failed effort using U.S. ground troops in South Vietnam. Such CIA officials as Bill Lair and Vint Lawrence, who originally set up the Hmong Army as a small-scale

5. Leaders justified their bombing of northern Laos by claiming they were defending Laos from a massive North Vietnamese invasion of more than 50,000 troops aimed at "taking over" Laos. In fact, as revealed by Noam Chomsky in his chapter on Laos in *At War with Asia* (New York: Pantheon, 1970), the evidence never showed more than a few thousand such troops in northern Laos between 1964 and 1969, when the people of the Plain of Jars were bombed, and the troops' main role was clearly defensive in nature. The United States imported far more Thai, National Chinese, and other foreign mercenary troops into Laos, and used northern Laos to attack neighboring North Vietnam. The radar site at Phou Pha Thi in northern Laos was used to guide bombers into North Vietnam, and the CIA used its local troops to conduct espionage, sabotage, and assassination missions into North Vietnam. The North Vietnamese were almost entirely focused on their effort to win in South Vietnam and clearly had no intention of "taking over" Laos since they could have done so at any point during or after the war had they wished to do so. This is proven today by the fact that North Vietnam did withdraw their troops from Laos after the war ended, and the main players in the Laotian economy today are Thailand and China.

guerrilla effort, were appalled when CIA chief Ted Shackley took over the war in 1966 and vastly expanded it, leading to the decimation of the Hmong. The U.S. attitude toward the Hmong was later explained by Air Force General Heinie Aderholt when he stated on camera in the film *The Ravens: Covert War in Laos* that, "It's easier to lose your Hmong people than to lose Americans. It doesn't make as bad publicity at home."

Shackley's tenure saw the CIA take control of the targeting for the bombing and not only escalate it but direct it at destroying civilian targets in an attempt to compensate for the weakness of their "Secret Army" troops on the ground.

In the novel *Nineteen Eighty-Four*, George Orwell envisions a future in which leaders wage automated war involving "very small numbers of people, mostly highly-trained specialists," who fight "on the vague frontiers whose whereabouts the average man can only guess at." In the 1960s, that future was realized in Laos.

To this day, few people outside Laos have any inkling of what occurred on the Plain of Jars between 1964 and 1969. These voices from the Plain of Jars thus reveal that Orwell's prophecy became reality during these years.

How This Book Came to Be

I awoke in the capital city of Vientiane, Laos, on a day in early September 1969 with no idea that my life was about to change forever.

I had arrived in Laos in March 1967, two and a half years earlier, at age twenty-five. I was employed by International Voluntary Services (IVS) as an educational adviser. After completing my assignment as a teacher in Tanzania from 1965–67, I had decided to go to Laos both because I believed deeply that education should seek to develop rural villages and because I was seeking to retain my "2A" draft status to avoid being drafted to fight in a war that I opposed. Working with IVS, which was funded by the U.S. Agency for International Development (USAID), I spent most of my time (a) writing a textbook (which was never used) to teach basic agricultural principles to elementary school children and (b) sending future teachers to train in community development in Thailand.

After arriving in Laos, I decided to live in a Lao village. Though only 11 kilometers (6.8 miles) outside Vientiane, the village lacked running water and electricity. I learned to speak Laotian and finished my alternative to military service three months before discovering the bombing. I remained because I really liked Laos and Lao people and was at loose ends about what to do next.

My years in the village had led me to deeply appreciate Lao rice farmers. I neither idealized nor romanticized them, and had certainly met some I disliked. But, on the whole, I had never met a group of people whom I liked and respected more. I found them kind, friendly, cheerful, decent, fun, honest, sincere, and trustworthy. I appreciated how the villagers looked me in the eye, told the truth, and connected on a deep human level. Other people in this world may be as fine, I used to tell my friends, but I could not imagine any finer.

I felt particularly close to Paw Thou Douang, the village elder in whose house I lived. He was a deeply devout Buddhist and lay leader of the Buddhist temple ten yards from our home. He was also a medic, a farmer, and as I discovered after the war ended, the local representative of the Pathet Lao. He was a cheerful, kind, wise, gentle, and much-loved man whom I deeply respected, and he became a kind of second father to me.

Laos was then divided into the U.S.-supported Royal Lao Government zone of some two million people where I lived and the guerrilla Pathet Lao zone that contained some one million people and that was closed to Westerners. I was staying that day downtown with my friend Tim Allman, a *New York Times* journalist, who asked me if I would interpret for him as he went to interview refugees from the Plain of Jars. The first residents of guerrilla zones ever to reach Vientiane, they were being housed at the That Louang pagoda in the center of the city.

I eagerly agreed. Although the Plain was only some 230 miles from Vientiane, it might as well have been on the other side of the moon for all we knew of it. I was curious about life in Pathet Lao zones and the rumors of bombing denied by the government but reported in *Le Monde* the previous spring.

Tim hopped on the back of my motorcycle. We drove up to That Louang and entered a large but sparsely furnished prayer shed the size of a football field, filled with hundreds of refugees spread out on the floor.

We picked one man at random and began to interview him in Laotian. When I asked him whether he had seen any bombing, his face clouded over, and he began to describe being bombed frequently for the previous five years. At one point he crouched down and did something that has remained engraved in my memory ever since. He drew an "L" in the dust, showing the shape of the shelter he had dug into the side of a mountain. There he had hidden during the day for months on end to escape the bombers that came every day and gradually demolished his entire village. "We lived like animals," he said, explaining how he could come out only at night to try to do some farming and find some food to keep himself and his family alive.

Shaken by these revelations, I then interviewed more than a dozen refugees. Every one gave the same basic report. The bombing had begun in 1964, gradually intensified year by year until, starting in late 1968, they were bombed daily. Villager after villager described seeing relatives and friends burned and buried alive, their livestock killed, and their homes and pagodas demolished; living in holes for months on end; and feeling intense pain at being forcibly removed from the villages of their ancestors to wind up as penniless refugees in Vientiane. Having lived in a Lao village, I could imagine their intense pain at being separated from the beloved villages of their birth. Their practice of paying homage to ancestors at village and home shrines, with an expectation that their own descendants would one day perform the same rituals for them, was central to their psychological and spiritual well-being.

But it was only as I went back frequently to talk with the refugees over the next fifteen months—and then view the drawings and read the essays that appear in this book—that I began to fully understand the deep humanity of these people, what they had been through, and the implications of their experiences for all humanity.

The refugees in That Louang were soon moved out to camps around Vientiane. Over the next six months, more were brought from the north, and the number of refugees from the Plain grew to some twenty-five to thirty thousand people. During the months of interviewing them, I realized that these people had been bombed for more than five years without outsiders, including even those of us living in Laos, knowing that the bombing had occurred. Meanwhile, the U.S. government denied that it was doing any bombing in Laos at all. And, unlike in South Vietnam, journalists were not permitted to go out on bombing runs. It seemed eerie, frightening, and thoroughly unjust that a handful of leaders, both Democrats and Republicans alike, had the power to bomb masses of innocent civilians so secretly, massively, and destructively.

It was particularly disturbing to see the casualties of the bombing with my own eyes. I interviewed thirty-eight-year-old Thao Vong, a gentle father of four, who had been blinded by the bombing. I saw a young boy missing a leg. I spoke with the father of three-year-old Khamphong and saw his daughter, one of six of his children who was hit by cluster bombs on February 28,

1969, and felt the pellets still in her body. I learned from Pha Sii how her daughter-in-law was killed in August 1969 shielding her year-old child with her body. I met a thirty-five-year-old man from Ban Na Sou whose father, mother, wife, and three children were all killed in a July 15, 1967, bombing raid. I talked with Po Sing Som's wife, who described how her husband, in his sixties, was killed by antipersonnel bombs in a September 16, 1968, raid that wounded her and also left pellets still visible in her body.

As I collected information, two incidents stood out above all. One day in the camp, a mother gave me a photo of a sweet-faced woman named Sao Doumma, who would be killed in a bombing raid seven years later. The photo made a huge impression on me and came to symbolize the humanity of the unseen and unknown victims of the bombing. (The photo appears on this book's cover.) The second incident was meeting the mother of a three-year-old girl who had been burned on her breast, stomach, and vagina. When I returned a week later, I learned that the child had died.

It was during those months that I first learned of cluster munitions, or "antipersonnel" bombs, as air-force personnel called them. One day I saw one in a hut; a yellow pineapple bomb, from which the explosive powder had been removed, fashioned into a lamp. The refugees said it was bombs like these they most feared. Their pellets could not destroy structures but could and did deeply pierce the flesh, entering in a zigzag pattern that made them hard to remove, in the unlikely event that one could reach a doctor. Exploding on impact over a wide area, cluster bombs killed or maimed those who could not dive into their holes fast enough, particularly older people who were slower at running or children confused by the noise and smoke. Even after the bombing stopped, the danger was still present in the thousands of unexploded bomblets scattered across the Plain. These continued to explode if stepped upon, even when the bombing had stopped. I later learned that each bombing sortie carried 1,000 bomblets, and each bomblet had 200 to 260 ball-bearing pellets. That meant that one bombing sortie blanketed a village with 200,000 to 260,000 pellets designed to maim not kill. Fighter-bombers flew 541,738 bombing stories in Laos, the great majority of which—according to air-force personnel—dropped cluster bombs.

And the bombing had not stopped. At that very moment, I realized, Lao people alive today would be bombed to death tomorrow. I am Jewish, and had been deeply moved when meeting Holocaust survivors some years earlier. In Laos I realized that I had discovered a crime as unacceptable as

Auschwitz—while the unprovoked murder of civilians was still going on. Without any conscious decision, I soon found myself committed to doing whatever I could to stop the bombing by trying to expose it to the world.

Only a handful of reporters were permanently stationed in Laos. Most journalists of note came in from elsewhere to report for a week at a time. Over the next fifteen months, I wound up working for reporters from all of the major TV networks and from many of the newspapers, including Bernie Kalb of CBS News, Ted Koppel of ABC News, Welles Hangen of NBC News, Sydney Schanberg and Flora Lewis of the *New York Times*, and many others. From their perspective, they were hiring an interpreter and guide. From mine, I was trying to get the story of the bombing on TV and in newspapers back in the United States. I also took photos of, and tape-recorded conversations with, the refugees and sent them to Senators Kennedy and Fulbright, escorted visiting peace activists like Noam Chomsky out to the camps, and briefed diplomats and congressional aides.

During this period I became friendly with a Plain of Jars refugee who was my age. His name was Ngeun. He stood out for his obvious intelligence, cheerfulness, warm-heartedness, self-confidence, honesty, and steadfastness. Ngeun became the closest friend I have ever had, and I learned that he had been a former soldier, cadre, and medic for the Pathet Lao.

It was Ngeun who collected the essays and drawings that appear in this book. He did so at some risk, as he had to hide them under his shirt as he passed through police checkpoints.

When I returned to Washington, DC, in February 1971, I brought the essays and drawings with me. Although I spoke Laotian, I did not read it. So the essays sat in my closet for six months until I contacted a Lao student in Montreal named Hiem Phommachanh who agreed to help me translate them. Hiem, now the Minister of Post, Telecom, and Communication, would translate the essays aloud from Laotian into French, and I would type them up in English. I find it moving today to remember how, while the U.S. government was continuing to murder Laotians in Southeast Asia, an American and a Lao citizen worked for weeks in my small room, deeply absorbed in our collaboration, feeling much the same horror and sadness, and determined that these distant voices would be heard.

Voices from the Plain of Jars: Life under an Air War was published in the summer of 1972 and received widespread critical acclaim. *New York Times* columnist Anthony Lewis wrote that:

[Ambassadors] Sullivan and Godley . . . played a decisive part in what must qualify as the most appalling episode of lawless cruelty in American history, the bombing of Laos. . . . The human results of being the most heavily bombed country in the history of the world were expectably pitiful. They are described without rancor—almost unbearably so—in a small book that will go down as a classic. It is "Voices From the Plain of Jars," . . . in which the villagers of Laos themselves describe what the bombers did to their civilization. No American should be able to read that book without weeping at his country's arrogance.[6]

Material from the book also appeared on numerous television shows, such as the *CBS Evening News* with Walter Cronkite and a Bill Moyers TV show, in which the drawings were displayed and their captions read. Book material also appeared widely in the media, including in the entire *New York Times* op-ed page on July 16, 1971, and in publications by the peace movement. The book did not sell many copies, however. I found then, and ever since, that Americans have little interest in or concern for the suffering of their leaders' victims, whom they treat as "nonpeople."

ERA OF THE BLUE MACHINE

The other major dimension of my work after learning of the bombing in Laos in September 1969 was to investigate the automated war I had discovered. One of my first reactions to discovering the bombing was absolute bewilderment. Who had ordered this horror? How had it happened? Where were the bombers coming from? Who was in charge of them? Why had they decided to so massively target old people, women, and children? How could they be so indifferent to human life? I set out to find out.

During the next fifteen months I visited air bases in Thailand and South Vietnam and interviewed a wide variety of personnel involved in the bombing—including pilots, ordnance experts, and the former Air Force captain in charge of target selection at the U.S. Embassy in Vientiane. Nothing struck me so much during this period as the contrasts: those (a) between the reports of the Lao refugees and those of the pilots bombing them, death and destruction below while pilots above returned to their air bases in Thailand for a cold one and carousing in the bars at night, (b) between the countries

6. Anthony Lewis, "Another Senate Test," *New York Times,* July 9, 1973.

with the world's most sophisticated technology and the poverty-stricken villages that had that technology deployed against them, and (c) between the on-the-ground horror felt by the gentle Lao rice farmers who were forced to live in holes like animals for years and the technocratic, cold, and inhuman indifference of those in power who had destroyed their lives.

On the one hand, guerrilla zones in Laos were composed of three to four thousand tiny villages—each consisting of a few dozen bamboo homes, a pagoda, rice storehouses, a few hundred head of water buffalo, and some cows, pigs, chickens, and ducks—and inhabited by some of the poorest, most gentle rice farmers in Southeast Asia. They enjoyed neither running water nor electricity. Most villagers were subsistence-level farmers who had to grow or catch the food they ate in order to survive. I still remember my shock back in 1967 when, about to travel to Laos, I opened the World Almanac to find its per capita income. There was only an asterisk indicating that Laos was a subsistence-level economy.

And every day for nine years, hundreds of millions of dollars of the world's most sophisticated aircraft were hovering over these poverty-stricken villages. The aircraft included 01E, 02, and OV10 spotter planes at two thousand feet; A-1E, A-26, and T-26 prop bombers and AC-47, AC-54, AC-119, and AC-130 gunships, flare ships, and rescue and gunship helicopters at five thousand feet; F-4, F-100, F-105, A-7, and B-57 jet bombers and jet reconnaissance and EC-47 and EC-119A electronic aircraft at ten thousand feet; KC-135 supertankers at twenty thousand feet; B-52s at thirty thousand feet; EC-130 command and control aircraft at thirty-five thousand feet; and SR-71 reconnaissance aircraft at seventy thousand feet.

Giant computers, seismic and acoustic sensors, infrared devices, and ANAPQ108 radar (designed to see through trees) tracked farmers trying to grow rice at night; laser-guided bombs and TV-guided missiles were loosed on buffalo, trucks, rice storehouses, homes, and peasants alike. More than two million tons of ordnance were dropped, and more than $10 billion was spent—$70 billion in today's dollars.[7]

At the time, I lived in a Lao village near Vientiane. The village was much like the villages on the Plain of Jars in that it lacked electricity, running water, and toilets. It was quite a contrast to go from my village to the giant air bases in Thailand and South Vietnam. Only as one drove past the paddy fields

---

7. "Indochina War Statistics—Dollars and Deaths," 14262 ff.

and samlor drivers onto an American air base in Indochina did one begin to appreciate the vast might deployed against the rice-farmers of the Plains of Jars.

Miles of roads stretched as far as the eye could see (an aviator, perhaps apocryphally, was said to have measured the roads on Korat Air Force Base and estimated that there were enough roads to make a two-lane highway to Peking and back). There were thousands of prefab structures, Quonset huts, trailers, tents, and wooden and cement buildings; acres of hospitals, commissaries, canteens, nightclubs, restaurants, swimming pools, barracks, gasoline pumps, garages, buses, trucks, jeeps, radios, radar installations, warehouses, offices, and hangars; millions of gallons of fuel on the "fuel farm"; and closed-circuit TV and radio and giant movie theaters.

Thousands of American and Asian personnel drove, scurried, and lolled about: pilots, radio operators, mechanics, bomb-loaders, fuse-installers, "fuel farmers," gas-pump operators, drivers, electricians, carpenters, janitors, doctors, medical orderlies, lawyers, chaplains, cooks, MPs, guards, loaders, stackers, waiters, "hooch-girls," secretaries, clerks, information officers, launderers, photo interpreters, gunners, navigators, and those wearing the uniforms of the Air Force, Navy, Marines, and Army and of Air America, Continental Air Service, Pan American, and Northwest airlines.

And then there were the planes constantly taxiing, taking off, flying, and landing—sleek, squat, giant, tiny, silver, and camouflage green.

And finally, of course, the ordnance—warehouses filled with the world's most destructive bombs and missiles short of nuclear weapons.

Five such installations existed in South Vietnam, with some forty thousand American aviators; another five installations were in Thailand, with twenty-five thousand aviators; four to six aircraft carriers operated in and out of the Gulf of Tonkin, with some ten to twenty thousand personnel; and a dozen smaller directed bases operated throughout Indochina for indigenous air forces.

And these installations were but a small part of what was then known as the Air Force's "Blue Machine," in contrast to the Army's "Green Machine." The Air Force logistics network stretched from 18 major air bases in the Pacific to 112 in the United States and provided the personnel and planes necessary to keep the bombs falling.

But perhaps the greatest contrast for me was between the voices of the refugees and those of the pilots. When I was talking with a pilot in Saigon,

I remembered how gentle Thao Vong, the thirty-eight-year-old rice farmer who had been blinded in an air raid, had described the horror his life had become. It was chilling to hear how cold and bloodlessly the pilots described their role in ruining his life. "I'm as liberal, as much for peace as anyone else. But war is not a pretty thing. In a guerrilla war, the civilians are going to pay a price. War has now progressed to a point where you're going to bomb civilian targets and that's it. I'll be frank. I'm trained to kill people. I don't like it particularly. But when the time comes, I'm prepared to do it."[8]

I thought of the Lao mother of that three-year-old girl who had died from the napalm burns to her breasts, stomach, and vagina as a pilot at Da Nang Air Base proudly informed me, "Our 500-pound nape canisters are newer; they have a better dispersal pattern than the older 1,000 pounders."

I then listened in shock as the Air Force information officer told the pilot, "Hey, you're not supposed to talk about the napalm."

"No shit. Why not?" the pilot asked.

"Well, you know those college kids," the information officer explained. "Pretty soon they're going to put poor Dow Chemical out of business. You're not supposed to talk about it to the press."

"Well," the pilot responded, "it seems pretty ridiculous to me that people can be so emotional about how you kill people. What's so bad about nape anyway?"

And I thought of sweet-faced Sao Doumma as a pilot also told me, "My way of killing people is better than, than, their way. The Pathet Lao and North Vietnamese are a plague. We have to eliminate them. They have no regard for human life."

Two moments, however, struck me the most during that visit to Da Nang Air Base. The first occurred when I asked a group of pilots if they ever got any feedback about the people killed in action as a result of their raids. Suddenly, the room became alive with feeling, in stark contrast to the polite but detached tones they had been talking in until then.

The men in the room began to chuckle, as one pilot explained: "You've hit on a rather sore point, you know. You could say there's kind of a controversy between us and the grunts on that subject." He then went on to explain that the pilots felt that the foot soldiers were taking credit for aerially inflicted casualties.

8. Pilot interviews cited here were conducted at Da Nang Air Base in South Vietnam in November 1970.

The pilots grew increasingly indignant as they told personal anecdotes of having been "robbed" of "kills." A typical example was given by the pilot who exploded:

One day we went in over a North Vietnamese military camp on top of a mountain. It was right out in the open, so we could see it and everything. We plastered the place, napalm, 500-pounders, the works. I know we had kills; you could see people running all over the place, buildings burning. There was no way for there to be no KIA. But do you know what happened? The grunts came in and reported twenty-five enemy killed by ground fire. All they did was shoot their M-16s into the corpses and then claim they'd killed them. The nerve. Can you imagine?

Of course, the last place the North Vietnamese would build a "military camp" would be on top of a mountain easily visible from the air.

The second unforgettable moment at Da Nang occurred when I was taken out to the flight deck to see airplanes about to take off to bomb Laos. I was struck by how the pilots had decorated the nose of the planes with shark teeth, much in the way that many had, no doubt, decorated their autos as teenagers just a few years earlier. As I stood there, thinking of the tens of thousands of Lao peasants at that very moment living in caves and holes, terrified of being killed, one of the pilots suddenly stuck out his hand and said, "Well, wish me luck!" I shook it numbly.

I was struck above all by the banality of the evil in most of my conversations with the pilots. One fellow informed me cheerfully that "it may sound trite, but it's the only war we've got. Do you realize this is the only place in the world right now where you can drop live bombs?" Another was even more upbeat as he explained, "The Russians are going nuts over what we're learning out here. They're dying that they can't test their stuff out." And another explained:

The whole problem comes from Kennedy's "flexible response" idea. You hit me on the foot; I hit you on the ankle. You hit me on the knee; I hit you on the shin. But it doesn't work. If you hit me on the foot, I should slug you with a club and put you out of commission. I'm not saying we were right. Let's face it, we just attacked the fuckers. But when we did decide to bomb them, we should have kicked the shit out of them.

It was this contrast between the Lao voices I heard in the refugee camps and those who were destroying their lives that seemed most significant to me. I realized that the automated war over Laos changed not only the mechanics but the psychology of warfare. In this new era, tens of thousands of innocents who were killed or wounded were not even regarded as human beings, their lives worth no more than those of chickens, pigs, or water buffalo.

CROSSROADS AND BATTLEGROUND, CA. 1250–1964

The Plain of Jars is located in the Laotian province of Xieng Khouang, one of Southeast Asia's most fabled, fought-over, and prosperous regions.

The province covers an area of more than 7,600 square miles, stretching from the border of North Vietnam to the north to the edges of the Mekong Valley to the south. It is a rich and beautiful area of soaring mountains, thick forests, and fertile valleys, with a fresh and bracing climate.

By the late 1950s, its population was estimated between 130,000 and 170,000.[9] Although fragmented into dozens of tribes and clans, most outsiders have divided them up into four major groups: 30,000 to 40,000 Kha peoples; another 30,000 to 40,000 Hmong and Yao tribespeople; 5,000 to 10,000 Vietnamese and Chinese; and some 65,000 to 80,000 Laotians.

The Kha are among the earliest inhabitants; descended from Mon-Khmer stock, they generally inhabit the mountain slopes between the Hmong above and the Lao below.

The Hmong and Yao are hill tribespeople from southern China who began coming into Xieng Khouang in the late 1850s. Arriving so late, they had to settle for living on the tops of Xieng Khouang's mountains. As a result, they developed a nomadic existence, practicing a slash-and-burn style of agriculture that necessitated their moving every five to seven years when the land was exhausted. Despite this, they managed to accumulate some wealth by learning to cultivate opium. They also distinguished themselves by keeping their rather well-developed cultures intact.

The Vietnamese and Chinese were last to arrive, mostly during the twentieth century. They made up most of the population of the region's major towns and provided the backbone of the commercial and administrative infrastructure.

9. Frank M. LeBar and Adrienne Suddard, eds., *Laos: Its People, Its Society, Its Culture* (New Haven, CT: Human Relations Area Files, 1960), 238.

But the Laotians were the dominant group. Part of the Tai-speaking peoples stretching from southern China to the Gulf of Thailand, formerly the Gulf of Siam. They are believed to have come from China into northern Laos early in the first millennium after the birth of Christ. Settling in the rich mountain valleys, they established farming communities based on the cultivation of paddy rice. In time they diversified by growing a wide variety of vegetables and fruits, as well as by raising livestock. Their recorded history began about 1250. By the middle of the twentieth century, the Laotians of Xieng Khouang formed the political, cultural, and economic heart of the region. Their language was taught in the schools their children attended, and they staffed the civic administration. Known locally as the Lao Phoueun, their art, architecture, literature, handicrafts, and music were regarded as among the purest expressions of the ancient civilization of Laos.

The Plain of Jars was the heart of the Lao Phoueun civilization. The area takes its name from the large clay receptacles found there, which are believed to be the funeral urns of an ancient and long-forgotten Mon-Khmer race. The Plain itself is an elevated, sparsely inhabited, and grassy tableland, used mainly for grazing cattle and as a passage to other parts of the province. When Lao Phoueun speak of the Plain of Jars, they usually mean just this limited area. But most outsiders, including ourselves, use the name to refer to central Xieng Khouang province, the general area composed of the districts Muong Pek and Muong Khoun. It is an elevated plateau with gentle rolling hills, forests, and level farming land, and includes the area of the jars. The Plain was inhabited by approximately fifty to sixty thousand people in the late 1950s. About 80 percent were Lao Phoueun, 10 percent Chinese and Vietnamese, and another 10 percent or so Hmong and Kha tribespeople.

The Plain of Jars area was the focal point for the province, including the major towns of Xieng Khouang, Khang Khay, and Phonesavan. Its broad, rolling valleys, passing between high mountains, and its extensive network of roads and paths leading from Vietnam into the Mekong Valley had long made the Plain a commercial entrepôt. Everything from opium to gold to cloth passed through the province to the peoples throughout Southeast Asia and beyond. Its cool climate, rich and well-watered soil, grassy savannah lands, and natural resources had also made it an economic prize. It had long been the largest fruit-producing and cattle-raising area of Laos. Salt and iron were mined here, and the Plain was believed to possess deposits of gold, copper, and sticklac as well. Its forests were as dense as any in Laos. And its beauty exerted a strange pull on both foreigners and local inhabitants alike. Correspondent Robert Shaplen, for example, visited the Plain after its destruction in September 1969 and wrote of its beauty amidst the devastation:

> The Plain, which is 3,500 feet above sea level, is unbelievably beautiful. Although the hot weather of the dry season sears it yellow, on the sunny day after a rainfall when I was there it was a magnificent emerald green savannah, except for a few undulating slopes and ravines with trees which cast oblique shadows. Pools of water glistened like broken mirrors. . . . Herds of cattle and wild ponies roamed the area, but except for one refugee camp the plateau was otherwise deserted. Xieng Khouang was mostly rubble, except for a pagoda, in the empty waste of which stood a large and a small Buddha; and Khang Khay was a shell of houses.[10]

Not only did the Plain's natural gifts make it an economic crossroads, but its fertile, elevated farmland valleys also made it an ideal invasion route, north or south. Located between the northern half of Vietnam and the Mekong Valley, the Plain was one of the most fought-over areas in Southeast Asia. For the Vietnamese, it was a potential rear base for attacks from the south across indefensible frontiers; similarly, those concerned with the Mekong Valley regarded the Plain as a possible springboard for an invasion from the north. From the beginnings of its recorded history, the Plains of Jars had been a major battleground, first for neighboring armies and then for great powers from across the sea.

The recorded history of the region may be divided into three main periods.

The feudal era, ca. 1250–1892: Its history during this time reads like a funeral lament for generation after generation of Lao Phoueun. One neighbor after another would war on the area, hold sway for a number of years, and then give way to a new set of conquerors. Innumerable groups of Cambodians, Burmese, Chinese hill tribes, Laotians from north or south, and, most frequently, Thais held power during this period.

The colonial period, 1893–1945: In 1893 the French took control, an event that signaled that the Plain's destiny was no longer determined by its immediate neighbors but by distant and more technologically advanced races.

10. Robert Shaplen, "Our Involvement in Laos," *Foreign Affairs* 48, no. 3 (April 1970): 488–89.

The French rule was distinguished by several local rebellions growing out of fairly widespread discontent with such measures as conscripted labor and taxes, and growing friction between the Hmong and Lao. But the French retained their hold on the Plain until its occupation by the Japanese during World War II.

The period of decolonization, 1946–1964: These years were marked by the withdrawal of the French from the Plain in 1954, post-1954 American intervention concentrating on wooing the Hmong, and the emergence of the Plain as a major Cold War battleground.

The French re-occupied the region in 1946 and used it as an air base, supply depot, and base camp until their defeat by Lao and Vietnamese guerrillas in 1954. From 1954 until 1960, the Plain was under the formal aegis of a series of pro-Western regimes based in the capital, Vientiane, and headed by Lao leaders who had sided with the French against the Lao and Vietnamese independence movements during the First Indochina War.

The Lao leadership had been badly split during this war. In the 1940s most of the leaders had been part of the Lao Issara independence movement directed against the Japanese. However, when the French moved in to retake Laos in late 1945, an extreme right-wing faction sided against the Lao Issara. In 1949, a moderate right-wing faction (headed by northern Prince Souvanna Phouma) set up a government under the French National Union. The moderate right-wing faction returned to Laos to fight with the French against the Vietminh. In 1950, anti-French Lao nationalists, headed by Souvanna Phouma's half-brother, Prince Souphanouvong, formed the Pathet Lao ("nation of Laos").

In 1954 moderate and extreme right-wing factions established a Royal Lao Government (RLG) in Vientiane. The Pathet Lao set up headquarters in the northeastern province of Sam Neua. The Plain of Jars, located midway between the two, became a major political and, later, military battleground.

In 1958 the Pathet Lao and a left-wing neutralist party aligned with them agreed to a special supplementary parliamentary election designed to integrate them into a representative RLG. But when they won thirteen out of twenty-one seats, the right-wing faction led by the CIA-supported General Phoumi Nosavan deposed Souvanna Phouma in May 1959 and imprisoned Souphanouvong and most of the other top Pathet Lao leadership. (However, they escaped from prison on May 23, 1960, and returned to Sam Neua.)

The principal Western actor during this period was the United States, whose activities included funding the Vientiane regimes (and far-right coups) at a cost of $480.7 million between 1955 and 1963; expanding the right-wing Lao army from a few thousand in 1954 to more than thirty thousand by 1960; creating a separate CIA-led "Secret Army" consisting of Hmong tribesmen and foreign mercenaries; and bringing in a CIA-owned airline, Air America. These actions gave the United States control and direction over Western activities in Xieng Khouang.

The creation of the Hmong army was the most far-reaching. During the late 1930s, the French had appointed Touby Lyfoung district administrator of the Hmong, choosing him over his cousin Faydang. In return, Touby sided with the French against the Lao Issara. By 1949 the Hmong had split into two warring factions, with Faydang, now a vice-chairman in the Pathet Lao, leading one of them. After 1954, the United States, through Touby and a then-unknown Hmong sergeant in the French Army named Vang Pao, created a Hmong paramilitary force independent of the Lao army to fight the Pathet Lao.

In July 1961, CIA Colonel Edward Lansdale reported to American Ambassador Maxwell Taylor in Vietnam that "about nine thousand Hmong tribesmen have been equipped for guerrilla operations, which they are now conducting with considerable effectiveness in Communist-dominated territory in Laos. Political leadership of the Hmong is officially in the hands of Touby Lyfoung, who now operate mostly out of Vientiane; the military leader is Lt. Col. Vang Pao, who is the field commander. Command control of Hmong operations is exercised by the chief C.I.A. Vientiane with the advice of Chief M.A.A.G Laos."[11]

By January 1961, however, the West had lost control of most of the Plain to an alliance of the Pathet Lao with the armies of the neutralist Kong Le, a former paratroop captain who had seized control of Vientiane in August 1960. Kong Le had joined with the Pathet Lao when the United States refused to support him after his coup. Within Xieng Khouang, United States influence shrank to the area southwest of the Plain, the site of a major military base, Long Tieng, where the CIA-directed Hmong army and their dependents were based.

11. Edward Lansdale, "Lansdale Memo for Taylor on Unconventional Warfare," Document 22, in *The Pentagon Papers* (New York: Bantam Books, 1971), 134–35.

Kong Le established an administration at Khang Khay, with Souvanna Phouma as prime minister. Kong Le and the Pathet Lao, both of them supported by the Soviet Union, continued to fight against the U.S.-supported Lao and Hmong armies until peace was established in July 1962. Souvanna Phouma then returned to Vientiane to head the Government of National Union, established as part of the 1962 Geneva Accords on Laos.

During 1963, Kong Le's alliance with the Pathet Lao began to crumble. Although Kong Le then turned to the United States for aid, what he received did not suffice to keep his troops intact. A faction of his army, headed by Colonel Deuane Sipraseuth, joined with the Pathet Lao; open warfare broke out between Kong Le and his rightists, on one hand, and the Pathet Lao and the Deuanists (Patriotic Neutralist Forces), on the other. Eventually, the Pathet Lao and Deuanists drove the rightist and Kong Le armies off the Plain in May 1964.

The West retained control of both the Long Tieng area and mountaintop Hmong villages in Xieng Khouang province, which were supplied by Air America. Starting in the early 1960s, however, increasing numbers of Hmong either had been brought out from their villages down to the Long Tieng area or had sought refuge there because of the fighting. The Pathet Lao controlled some 80 percent of Xieng Khouang's lowlands, from south and southwest of the Plain of Jars through the entire Plain area up to the borders of Sam Neua and Vietnam.

The Plain of Jars's era of decolonization had come to an end.

Automated Battlefield, 1964–1969

The Pathet Lao rule over the Plain of Jars begun in May 1964 brought its people into a postcolonial era. The refugees reported that, for the first time, the people of the Plain were taught pride in their country and people, instead of admiration for a foreign culture; schooling and massive adult literacy campaigns were conducted in Laotian instead of French; and mild but thorough social revolution—ranging from land reform to greater equality for women—was instituted.

There was relatively little North Vietnamese involvement during these years. There were some economic and military advisers from 1964 through 1968, though far fewer than the vast American aid apparatus in RLG zones. But, according to the refugees, the Vietnamese advisers lived apart and had little to do with the people of the Plain. As a bitterly anti-North Vietnamese

USAID worker wrote in a document widely distributed by the American Embassy in Laos: "the [North Vietnamese] cadres live apart from the Lao in self-imposed isolation they raise their own livestock, tend to their own gardens, and maintain discipline with their own self-criticism sessions."[12]

All told, by 1969, perhaps as many as several thousand North Vietnamese combat troops were fighting in Xieng Khouang.[13] This appears to have been a reaction to the heavy bombing and the ever greater numbers of Thai and Americans fighting in and over northern Laos, as well as to the American use of northern Laos for radar sites and espionage and assassination raids against North Vietnam.[14] The North Vietnamese were focused on their battle in South Vietnam against U.S. troops and used as few troops as possible in northern Laos.

May 1964, however, not only marked the beginning of a new era of nationalistic Lao rule for the people of the Plain. It also brought the first American bombers.

12. Edwin T. McKeithen, "The Role of North Vietnam Cadres in the Pathet Lao Administration of Xieng Khouang Province" (Vientiane, Laos: American Embassy, April 1970), 12.

13. Arthur J. Dommen, another strongly anticommunist expert on Laotian affairs, estimates that the North Vietnamese had no more than 2,860 men available for combat in all of Laos outside the Ho Chi Minh Trail area, as late as 1968. See Dommen's *Conflict in Laos* (New York: Praeger, 1971), 386.

14. From the late 1950s on, the United States has used northern Laos as a base for Hmong and American Special Forces to enter North Vietnam to engage in espionage, sabotage, and assassination. In the mid-1960s, the United States also established several radar sites in northern Laos to aid American bombers attacking North Vietnam. The most important of these was at Phou Pha Thi, a mountain in Sam Neua province seventeen miles from the border with North Vietnam. There was a radar station on the mountain, manned by Americans, that both vectored planes in on bombing missions over the north and frequently released the planes' bombs for them in darkness or clouds as part of the Commando Bolt program; Phou Pha Thi also had sophisticated radio communications and rescue helicopters on it. It was overrun in March 1968, and more than twenty Americans were killed. Na Khang, to the south, was used in similar ways and captured by the Pathet Lao in March 1969.

The United States also used northwestern Laos as a base for carrying out espionage missions into China. Based at Nam Yu, some twenty miles north of Houei Sai, teams of Yao tribesmen trained and controlled by the CIA would enter China on missions of several weeks duration, tapping telegraph and telephone lines, making contact with dissident tribesmen, and kidnapping Chinese citizens who would be brought to Laos for CIA interrogation. (See reports by Mike Morrow, available from *Dispatch News Service*, Washington, DC.)

For American policymakers found themselves faced with a new situation as a result of Pathet Lao victory on the Plain. On one hand, the United States remained committed to maintaining Western control of the Mekong Valley by weakening the Pathet Lao to the north as much as possible and to using northern Laos as a base for operations against North Vietnam. On the other hand, the United States could no longer rely on their ground strength to maintain a foothold in northern Laos. The American-supported Lao and Hmong right-wing armies were clearly weaker than the Pathet Lao and North Vietnamese. And large numbers of American ground troops could not be openly introduced for fear of creating a second front in the escalating Vietnam War—and because American policymakers did not wish to be accused of violating the 1962 agreements neutralizing Laos.[15]

Therefore, the decision was made to wage war against the Plain in secret, and mainly from the air. So a new kind of warfare was launched, one to which no people in history had ever before been subjected.

War in Xieng Khouang had always been waged by ground armies. But now, with the exception of small bands of Hmong sent in for espionage, sabotage, and assassination, and some periodic shelling with mortar on the western edges of the Plain, there was relatively little ground fighting from 1964 through 1969.

Before, outsiders had always sought to occupy and rule the Plain. This time, however, the United States had no plans for retaking the Plain until late 1969. The major goal of its air warfare was simply, in the words of a September 1970 Senate Subcommittee on Refugees staff report, "to destroy the social and economic infrastructure of Pathet Lao held areas."[16] This time war did not mean an attempt to supplant the Pathet Lao. Rather it was meant to hurt them by depriving them of local food supplies, disrupting transport and communications, killing off potential recruits and rice porters, demoralizing the civilian population, and eventually causing a refugee flow away from the Plain.

Before, the inhabitants had always managed to reach some kind of accommodation with those who came to wage war in their land. This time, accommodation was impossible. One cannot plead or negotiate with machines.

---

15. "Declaration and Protocol on the Neutrality of Laos," Geneva, Switzerland, July 23, 1962.

16. U.S. Congress, Senate, Committee on the Judiciary, *Refugee and Civilian War Casualty Problems in Indochina* (September 28, 1970), a staff report of the Subcommittee on Refugees and Escapees, 19.

Every day for five and a half years, the reconnaissance and electronic aircraft would film and track the people below; the jet and prop bombers would bomb them with white phosphorous, fragmentation, ball-bearing, and fléchette antipersonnel bombs and immediate and delayed-action high explosives; the gunships and spotter planes would strafe them with machine-gun fire.

Bombing sorties went from a daily half dozen or so in 1964 to dozens to hundreds per day by 1969. In May 1964, the bombing was carried out mainly by prop-driven planes striking mostly in the forest. By 1967, jets began to outnumber props, and villages were struck frequently, with the people start-ing to move underground or out into the forests. And after the November 1968 bombing halted over North Vietnam, the planes, which had been busy there, were diverted over the Plain, and virtually everything was destroyed.

The bombing was characterized above all by the heavy toll it took on the civilian population. In our interviews with more than one thousand Plain of Jars refugees, we recorded on film and tape dozens and dozens of case his-tories of villagers killed or wounded by the bombing. Refugees explained that much of this was because the children lacked discipline and the older people were often too infirm to reach a safe place fast enough. Relatively few soldiers were reported to have been struck by the bombs. Refugees explained that the troops hid deep in the forest and kept on the move con-stantly in small groups at night. They said that it was mostly civilians who were struck because families could not survive on the run and had to remain near the villages—which were the targets most often hit.

No one has described the nature of the bombing more clearly than the Belgian United Nations adviser Georges Chapelier. His carefully researched, in-depth study of refugees from the Plain explains that:

> Prior to 1967, bombing was light and far from populated centers. By 1968 the intensity of the bombings was such that no organized life was possible in the villages. The villagers moved to the outskirts and then deeper and deeper into the forest as the bombing climax reached its peak in 1969 when jet planes came daily and destroyed all stationary structures. Nothing was left standing. The villagers lived in trenches and holes or in caves. They only farmed at night. All of the interlocutors, without any exception, had his village completely destroyed. In the last phase, bombings were aimed at the systematic destruction of the material basis of the civilian society.

Harvests burned down and rice became scarce, portage became more and more frequent.[17]

An official United States Information Service survey, though phrased more blandly, confirmed these findings. Based on interviews with refugees from ninety-six Plain of Jars villages, it reported that:

Ninety-seven percent of the people said they had seen a bombing attack. Forty-nine percent said they could not count the number of times they had seen bombs dropped and 43 percent said they had seen planes bomb "frequently." Sixty-eight percent of 168 responses tabulated indicated that the respondents had seen a person killed. That the bombing raised havoc with the lives of the people while they were in the Plain of Jars area is not to be denied. Ninety-nine percent of the 212 respondents said the bombing made life difficult for them. Eighty-seven percent reported building a shelter in the woods after they first saw a bombing raid. The bombing is clearly the most compelling reason for moving.[18]

And a State Department summary of the same survey added that "ninety-five percent of the 169 persons who responded to the question said their villages had been bombed." It also explained that "two thirds had seen someone injured by the bombs; in 80 percent of such cases the victim was a villager, in 20 percent the victim was a Pathet Lao."[19]

Between April and August 1969, the people of the Plain came under the most intense bombing since it had begun in May 1964. The Pathet Lao withdrew, taking the bulk of the young people and many civilians with them. Hmong soldiers of the Secret Army then occupied the Plain and evacuated twenty to thirty thousand civilians to several refugee camps, ringing the capital city of Vientiane.

By September, the society of fifty thousand people living in and around the area no longer existed. History had conferred one last distinction upon it: The Plain of Jars had become the first society to vanish through automated warfare.

17. George Chapelier, "Plain of Jars: Social Changes under Five Years of Pathet Lao Administration," *Asia Quarterly*, 1971/1, Universite Libre de Bruxelles, Belgium, pp. 18–19, p. 36.

18. U.S. Congress, *War-Related Civilian Problems in Indochina*, 17–18.

19. Ibid., 15.

THE SURVIVORS, 1969–1975 AND BEYOND

The aftermath of the Plain's destruction brought continuing hardship to its survivors. Most of the youth, fifteen to twenty thousand in number, retreated with the Pathet Lao to continue their lives under the bombs. The five thousand or so Chinese and Vietnamese, their loyalties doubted by the CIA, were immediately flown to Vientiane, where they were forced to start their lives over again as peddlers, waiters and waitresses, and maids and coolies. Some two thousand of the young Lao men, mostly the last remaining sons in their families, who had been left behind by the Pathet Lao to help their parents and younger siblings, were forced to join the Hmong army to fight against their brothers and sisters on the other side. Placed in the most exposed positions on the front lines by Hmong leaders bent on revenge, they have suffered an enormously high casualty rate.

The remaining people from the Plain of Jars, some twenty to thirty thousand Lao Phoueun adults and children, were first placed in refugee camps in the mountains around the Long Tieng area. There they were ravaged by epidemics, and a great many of them, mostly children, died. In one camp, for example, refugees reported that three hundred persons had died out of a total population of twelve hundred. In September 1969 the first refugees were brought down to Vientiane, while in November 1969 some fifteen thousand Plain of Jars refugees were shifted up on the Plain again in an abortive attempt by the CIA to create two strategic hamlets.

When it became clear that the Pathet Lao were going to counterattack the Plain anyway, these people were airlifted down to the Vientiane Plain in February 1970. There they were placed in nearly two dozen camps scattered in a fifty mile radius of the capital city of Vientiane. During the course of the next year, another ten to fifteen thousand who had remained behind at Long Tieng came down into the Vientiane camps on foot and by vehicle, bringing the total population of the camps today to some twenty-five to thirty thousand.

Their lives in these camps were very difficult. When the Hmong captured the Plain in April and August 1969, they had taken revenge on the villagers. They burned whatever shelters and belongings remained, and either stole or slaughtered their water buffalo, cows, pigs, and chickens before their eyes. Thus the people from the Plain arrived in the refugee camps with virtually nothing.

In addition, they were unable to purchase food, livestock, tools, or medicine with the Pathet Lao currency they held. For although Lao officials at Long Tieng had promised to replace this currency with bills negotiable in Western-controlled zones, this pledge was not honored.

In Vientiane, they were given some of the poorest land in the province and told to farm it. Most of this land was uncleared. Lacking livestock, they were reduced to trying to clear it by hand, and had but meager success. The yields on the little land they were able to clear, moreover, were minimal. Up on the Plain, they were used to growing rice in water-filled paddies. Down in Vientiane, they could grow only upland rice, which depended on the little rainwater their rather porous land could hold. Insects also proved a problem. And so, in Vientiane their yields were but a tiny fraction of what they were once able to grow back home.

Lacking money and livestock, unable to grow or buy food, they were forced to subsist on American handouts of rice and salt, the few fish they could catch from nearby streams, or the leaves they could pick in the forests.

This poor diet, coupled with the hot climate of the Vientiane Plain, resulted in medical problems ranging from malnutrition to disease. Medical care was minimal. Some dispensaries were set up by USAID, but in general they were woefully understocked. And the Lao doctors and staff often insisted on illegally charging the refugees for what Western-donated medicine there was, while making little attempt to care for the people. Some Western medical teams in private programs did visit the camps, but their efforts did not begin to meet the need.

A Government Accounting Office team dispatched to the camps by a United States Senate subcommittee on refugees in September 1970 reported an abnormally high death rate among the Plain of Jars refugees. Little attempt was made to alleviate it.[20]

Not surprisingly, the survivors of the bombing and destruction of the Plain of Jars had little desire to remain where they were. They talked constantly of their distaste for the hot climate, their lack of land and means of livelihood, of what they had lost, and of the one simple thing they wished to regain—returning home.

20. Ibid., 63. Information on this period is available from the Mennonite Central Committee, at http://clusterbombs.mcc.org/.

We visited a dozen different camps making up 60 percent of the total refugee population from the Plain of Jars; we went out to these camps nearly one hundred times; we spoke with more than one thousand people.

And in each camp, each time, each person confided to us but one basic wish: to return to the village of his or her birth.

When the war ended in 1975, many of the refugees achieved their wish and were allowed to return to the Plain of Jars. When they did so, however, they discovered that it had become a hellscape of unexploded cluster bombs, which were to kill twenty thousand more innocent civilians after the war ended. According to American workers for the Quaker and Mennonite Central Committee who visited the Plain frequently, the unexploded bombs caused those who returned to live in fear and denied them access to land they desperately needed in order to survive.

U.S. leaders have cleaned up only 0.28 percent of the 80 million unexploded cluster bombs they left behind in Laos. As a result, there are probably no people on earth who have been so tormented for so long by U.S. warmaking—as of 2013 it will be forty-nine years and counting.

You will read in this book how the people of the Plain of Jars suffered and died from bombing that went on between 1964 and 1973. Today their children, grandchildren, and great-grandchildren continue to suffer and die from U.S. bombs.

EXECUTIVE SECRET AUTOMATED WAR:
THE "LAOS MODEL"

During the seventeen months I spent investigating the bombing in Laos, from September 1969 until February 1971, I realized that U.S. Executive Secret Automated War represented an entirely new form of warfare.[21] And after returning to Washington, DC, in 1971, and following U.S. foreign and military policy for the next forty years, I found this insight has been borne out by events. Laos has been the model for increasing force projection abroad in many arenas. As U.S. leaders are forced to withdraw ground troops from Afghanistan and Iraq, the "Laos model" will be increasingly applied throughout the world.

21. Please see Fred Branfman, "Presidential War in Laos, 1964–70," in *Laos: War and Revolution,* ed. Nina S. Adams and Alfred W. McCoy (New York: Harper Colophon Books, 1970).

The three key features of this model are (1) unilateral U.S. Executive Branch power, independent of democratic control by Congress or the Judiciary, the media, or the public at large; (2) information management designed to keep executive war-making as much of a secret as possible from its own citizens and the world at large; and (3) increasing automated warfare, in which the killing is done by machines rather than by troops on the ground.

Unilateral Executive Branch Power

A handful of U.S. Executive Branch leaders began bombing northern Laos in May 1964, entirely on their own initiative. They did not inform Congress, as required by the Constitution. Nor did they inform the American public, meaning that they did not receive the "informed consent of the governed," also required by the Constitution. The bombing from 1964 until 1973 was conducted by both a Democratic Party administration—which dropped 454,200 tons on Laos—and a Republican administration, which dropped 1,628,900 tons.[22]

To understand the bombing of Laos, therefore, it is important to understand that the war in Laos was conducted by the Executive Branch as an *institution*. Giant Executive Branch agencies—the Defense Department, Pentagon, Air Force, Navy, CIA, National Security Council, and State Department—unilaterally conducted this war, entirely independent of democratic controls.

In August 1967, I accompanied two congressmen—Representative Lester Wolff (D-NY) and Representative Richard "Max" McCarthy (D-NY)—on a visit to Sam Thong, the showplace refugee center near the far larger CIA base at Long Tieng, which was designed to convince the world that the United States was involved only in helping refugees. As our plane approached Sam Thong, we were told that the runway there was muddy and we would have to land at an "auxiliary landing strip," thence to take a helicopter to Sam Thong. We did so, and, as the smiling congressmen proceeded down a line of welcoming Hmong, who draped them with Hawaiian leis, I walked over to a group of USAID officials who were talking with Edgar "Pop" Buell, the chief of USAID operations in Sam Thong. At one point Buell said to James Chandler, the deputy chief of USAID, "Do they know anything?"

22. "Indochina War Statistics—Dollars and Deaths."

Chandler responded, "Don't worry, Pop. [Deputy Chief of Mission] Hurwich gave them a beautiful snow job, complete with maps. They were very impressed."

Buell nodded, satisfied.

I later realized that the "auxiliary landing strip" was located at the CIA base of Long Tieng—whose existence was thus kept secret from these members and the rest of Congress. That night I shared a trailer with Congressman Wolff and encouraged him to find out more about the war in Laos. He grew agitated and said, with real fear in his voice, "Look, Fred, I was elected in 1964 on Lyndon Johnson's coattails. And if there's one thing we Democrats cannot do, it is to challenge LBJ!"

The Senate was informed for the first time that the United States was militarily involved in Laos in a closed session in the fall of 1968. Even then, however, ambassador to Laos William Sullivan and other Executive Branch officials lied to the Senate and did not inform senators of the massive bombing that was occurring.

The fall 1969 hearings were only held because it was no longer possible to keep U.S. military involvement in Laos and the Long Tieng base a secret after the first refugees were brought down from the Plain of Jars into Vientiane in September 1969. Although the hearings were closed, they were made public some months later.

At these fall 1969 hearings, Senator J. William Fulbright, the chairman of the Senate Foreign Relations Committee, revealed that Congress had been lied to a year earlier, expressing consternation that this was the first time the Senate had been informed of the extent of war-making in Laos. He stated: "I think the surprise that is evidenced by the chairman of the subcommittee and others, *that they did not know the extent of this involvement of these activities, though we had some hearings on it.* I do not know whether we know all of it now. I have no idea whether we do or not."[23]

Even after these October 1969 hearings, however, the Executive Branch continued to wage unilateral war in Laos with no meaningful congressional oversight.

23. U.S. Congress, Senate, Committee on Foreign Relations, *United States Security Agreements and Commitments Abroad: Kingdom of Laos* (October 20, 21, 22, and 28, 1969), in *Hearings before the Subcommittee on United States Security Agreements and Commitments Abroad,* 91st Cong., 1st sess., pt. 2 (Washington, DC: Government Printing Office, 1970), 547 (emphasis added).

A particularly dramatic example of unilateral executive power occurred in April 1971, at a hearing of the Senate Subcommittee on Refugees chaired by Senator Edward Kennedy. This hearing occurred in the wake of the winter 1971 South Vietnamese invasion of Laos, and the main Executive Branch witness was once again William Sullivan. President Nixon had finally admitted that the United States was bombing in Laos in March 1970, and so the main issue at this April 1971 hearing was not whether the United States was bombing Laos, but whether it had been bombing civilian targets.

After Ambassador Sullivan continued to lie, denying that the United States had been bombing civilian targets in Laos, Senator Kennedy called on me in the audience. I stood up, reported on what the refugees had told me, and ended by saying that "the evidence is overwhelming that the United States has been conducting the most protracted bombing of civilian targets in history."

When Kennedy then asked Sullivan about what I had said, Sullivan finally admitted that yes, civilians on the Plain of Jars had been bombed, but claimed that this was an exceptional case. At that point, Kennedy declared, "I don't believe you." The hearing ended. And the most massive bombing of civilians yet seen in Laos continued for another year and a half.

The true significance of this hearing is revealed by the fact that six months earlier, Senator Kennedy's own staff, after a visit to Laos, published a report stating that "the United States has undertaken a large-scale air war over Laos to destroy the physical and social infrastructure in Pathet Lao held areas. . . . Throughout all this there has been a policy of . . . secrecy. . . . The bombing has taken and is taking a heavy toll among civilians."[24]

At that official Senate hearing in April 1971 a representative of the Executive Branch thus looked a senator straight in the eye and blatantly lied to him. And, more significantly, that senator knew he was being lied to, given what his own staff had reported six months earlier. Had Ambassador Sullivan given sworn testimony to this committee, he would thus have committed perjury.

Yet Senator Kennedy took no action against Ambassador Sullivan or the Executive Branch for presenting what Kennedy knew to be false testimony. It was, for me, an iconic moment that symbolized the fact that the U.S. Executive Branch was an undemocratic institution, operating freely outside of Congressional or public control.

24. U.S. Congress, *Refugee and Civilian War Casualty Problems in Indochina*, 19.

The "Laos Model," therefore, features the unilateral use of Executive Branch military and CIA power, independent of democratic control, oversight, or even knowledge.

Strict Information Management—"Secret War"

Above, I have described the means by which the Executive Branch kept secret its dropping of more than two million bombs on Laos, many on civilian targets, for a nine-year period. The Executive Branch's strict information management system—first denying it was bombing in Laos at all, then denying that it was bombing civilian targets, and the whole time forbidding journalists from going on the bombing raids, unlike in South Vietnam—was an integral part of its bombing campaign and succeeded in its goals of giving the Executive as free a hand as possible to bomb when, how, and where they wished in Laos.

The goals of this Executive Branch secrecy included:

(1) Avoiding attempts by Congress to limit or influence the bombing campaign. Congress could hardly prevent a bombing campaign that it did not know about. Nor could it try to limit the bombing of civilian targets if the Executive Branch refused to release any information about these targets.

(2) Avoiding domestic public pressure by the peace movement to prevent or at least limit the bombing campaign. Allowing reporters to go out on bombing raids in South Vietnam produced some backlash against the bombing. Journalist Jonathan Schell's *The Village of Ben Suc*, for example, influenced many to oppose the war, including a young lieutenant named John Kerry, who went on to become the spokesperson for Vietnam Veterans Against the War, a senator, a presidential candidate, and head of the Senate Foreign Relations Committee. Denying the bombing of civilian targets in Laos, and refusing to allow journalists to witness the bombing, significantly reduced domestic public pressure against the bombing of Laos.

(3) Limiting the damage to America's international image that would have resulted had the world been aware of the massive bombing campaign being conducted against innocent civilians in Laos and the massive violations of international laws protecting civilians in wartime.

(4) Freeing the Executive Branch to conduct automated war in post-Indochina arenas.

This policy was not entirely successful. When I returned to the United States in February 1971, at the height of the South Vietnamese invasion of Laos, I was able to brief members of Congress, appear on TV, publish many articles in magazines and newspapers, and give many speeches to peace movement audiences.[25] The latter were particularly meaningful because even the peace movement was largely unaware that bombing was continuing. Despite withdrawing ground troops from South Vietnam, President Nixon and his National Security Adviser Henry Kissinger were escalating a massive air war against civilian targets throughout Indochina. The information about the increase in the air war helped to energize a good deal of peace movement activity throughout 1971 and 1972.

On the whole, however, Executive Branch information management about its bombing campaign was largely successful. To this day, relatively few people know what occurred in Laos, and many histories of the Indochina War have almost entirely ignored writing about the most protracted bombing of civilian targets in world history.

Automated Warfare

> Vang Pao would move out, identify the enemy, pull back, and the airpower would come in.[26] (Major General Robert L. Petit, Deputy Commander 7th/13th Air Force, Udorn, Thailand)

The secret Executive Branch war in Laos marks the first time in history that a superpower waged a protracted war using machines rather than ground troops. Airpower had traditionally been used to support troops fighting on the ground. In Laos, however, the opposite was true. The bulk of the warfare was waged by American aircraft, with no ground troops involved at all, in an attempt to destroy the physical and social infrastructure in guerrilla zones.

When local—Hmong, Lao, mercenary—ground troops were involved, airpower was not meant to supplement their efforts. Rather the troops were

25. "One Day the Airplanes Came," *New York Times*, op-ed page, July 16, 1971.

26. U.S. Congress, Senate, Committee on Foreign Relations, *United States Security Agreements and Commitments Abroad: Kingdom of Thailand* (November 1969), in *Hearings before the Subcommittee on United States Security Agreements and Commitments Abroad*, 91st Cong., 1st sess., vol. 1, pt. 3, 11 (Washington, DC: Government Printing Office, 1970), 784.

used to supplement the air power—serving as "live bait" to try to draw enemy fire so that the bombing could locate and try to destroy the enemy or go into areas after bombs had destroyed them to take out refugees.

One of the most significant aspects of automated warfare revealed by the air war in Laos was its internal dynamic for escalation, unrelated to the situation on the ground.

The refugees had reported, and later research confirmed, that the bombing of Laos underwent a massive escalation starting in November 1968. It was after this time, as a refugee wrote, that the "planes came like birds; the bombs dropped like rain," leveling virtually every village on the plane, until "you could see only the red, red ground," a thirty-five-year-old female refugee added.

This vast escalation of bombing of civilian targets occurred because President Lyndon Johnson had declared a bombing halt over North Vietnam in November 1968, and had then simply diverted the planes into northern Laos. There was no military or strategic reason for doing so. It was simply because, as Deputy Chief of Mission Monteagle Stearns testified to the U.S. Senate Committee on Foreign Relations in October 1969, "Well, we had all those planes sitting around and couldn't just let them stay there with nothing to do."[27]

The use of machines for war-making in Laos appealed to Executive Branch leaders for five major reasons:

(1) Already overstretched with what were ultimately 550,000 ground troops in South Vietnam, Executive Branch leaders were reluctant to commit more ground troops to invading and occupying Laos. Mass bombing meant they could wage war without the many difficulties that using ground troops in Laos would have brought.

(2) Bombing as opposed to invading and occupying Laos was relatively cost-effective. Dropping two million tons of bombs over a nine-year period cost the United States roughly $10 billion, $70 billion in today's dollars, or roughly $8 billion a year. Invading and occupying Laos for a similar period would have cost a great deal more, as it has in Afghanistan today, where estimates of costs to the United States begin at $100 billion a year.

27. U.S. Congress, *United States Security Agreements and Commitments Abroad: Kingdom of Laos*, 484.

(3) As with information management, using machines rather than ground troops gave officials a freer hand to wage war as they wished in Laos. Invading Laos with ground troops would have brought with it more attempts at congressional oversight, more media reportage, and more public concern.

(4) Aerial warfare, conducted in secret, compared to ground warfare was far less likely to stimulate domestic protest at home. The My Lai Massacre in South Vietnam, revealed by soldiers, helped increase opposition to the war back home. Similar massacres in Laos regularly committed from the air were not protested since they were unseen and unknown.

(5) By the late 1960s the army in Vietnam was falling apart, with widespread drug use, officers being "fragged" (killed) by their own troops, and numerous refusals to obey orders. The advantages of relying on machines rather than on more soldiers were obvious, a trend that has now accelerated with the growing use of drone aircraft worldwide.

Although the air war did enormous damage to civilians as well as to the "physical and social infrastructure" in guerrilla zones, it ultimately failed in its major objective: preventing a Communist victory in Laos. U.S. Executive Branch leaders' waging automated war and committing mass murder of the innocent villagers of the Plain of Jars thus not only violated the U.S. Constitution, international law, and the most basic codes of human decency. It demonstrated military incompetence and the falsehood of the claim that this kind of warfare actually protects U.S. national security.

Voices from the Plain of Jars

Our lives became like those of animals desperately trying to escape their hunters. . . . Human beings whose parents brought them into the world and carefully raised them with overflowing love despite so many difficulties, these human beings would die from a single blast as explosions burst, lying still without moving again at all. And who then thinks of the blood, flesh, sweat, and strength of their parents, and who will have charity and pity for them? . . . In reality, whatever happens, it is only the innocent who suffer. And as for others, do they know all the unimaginable things happening in this war?

—a thirty-year-old woman refugee from the Plain of Jars

In the life of the people of Xieng Khouang, there was war which brought death to the population and made it impossible to work, to grow rice, and to earn a livelihood. As in this picture, where there were people working in the rice field, in the garden, in the village, who were shot by the airplanes. The earth was struck and many, many cows, buffaloes, horses, and chickens also died.

—a twenty-seven-year old

What sadness!

a twenty-year-old man, a traditional singer

What sadness! Formerly, the fragrance of ripening rice
would fill the rice fields
I would see flowers opening their blossoms
everywhere
in the forests
How beautiful it was for us!

And we would sing songs together that the Pathet Lao had taught us. They
were usually gay songs.

I used to sing the following song together with my friends in the forests
and fields.

This is the song:

The Beautiful Land of Laos

The land of Laos, the country of Laos
Built strong and prosperous by the Laotian people
From long ago
The splendor, the beauty of
The mountains and great forests,
So gorgeous to gaze upon
It is our sustenance and
We Laotians love this Lao country
As if it were a part of us
Beautiful land of Laos,
Beautiful country of Laos,

We are defending it against foreign invaders
The Lao people, together
In solid partnership helping each other bravely,
Are expressing their love of nation
They are guarding Laotian traditions,
So as to have peace with independence
And be united all together.

The composer of the above song was a girl of sixteen from Ban Nouao.

I am a young farmer, thinking of the past. Although the airplanes bombed my village, we would still sing together. Certain of us died like pigs, like dogs. They bombed everywhere without any of us ever seeing them. I am disturbed just thinking about it, and I will never ever forget it.

Much time has passed
Since I left the village of my ancestors
And now I am homeless,
Dwelling in Vientiane, a place of refuge
My heart is sad and cries out for my rice field and village,
All that which I had built with my own hands and made flourish
I have left the region of my birth,
My pagoda, my cows, my water buffalo
Everything is dead and gone, disappearing without a trace
Because of the airplanes that bombed the length and breadth of
    Xieng
The airplanes that caused me to lose all that I had
The airplanes that forced me out to the forest to burrow into the
    earth like a mouse or a mole
The airplanes that made me leave my loved ones,
Brothers and sisters, aunt and uncle
I am so far away now as I dream of my wide rice fields and gardens
Of all that I had labored over since coming into this world
Each spring my fellow villagers and I would work the land,
Helping one another till all had finished
Boys and girls together, we would transplant and sing gay songs
While the airplanes dropped bombs on us from high in the heavens
We had to be brave and finish our work as if we did not know fear,

Remaining outwardly calm though our hearts were torn with terror
   within
Thinking of our earth and rice fields, now overgrown with weeds,
My heart yearns after them
Remembering how in the harvesting season,
Men and women, old and young, would all reap our crops together
How when the airplanes would come, we would run for the holes
How when all was quiet once more, we would come out to work
   again
How singing gaily together, our voices would echo
Far and wide throughout the fields
What terrible sadness.
So many loved ones killed
Because of the huge bombs the airplanes rained down upon us
So many loved ones forced to leave their native villages,
Leaving behind spacious rice fields and gardens now turned to dust.

There was one rice farmer who was forty-eight years old. He was born in the region of Xieng Khouang in the same village as I. This old man had no children, he only had a wife. And he earned his living as a rice farmer. He had a house and cows and buffalo. One day there was a plane which came and dropped bombs on his house, but he was not at home. After that he went to look for a hole in the morning and he was shot by an airplane and died. There was a villager who saw him die. He called for his wife to go look. The wife of the man went and she cried. She was most sorry about this. She thought of her husband until she finally became sick. But we took good care of the old woman. In the year 1968, the lives of the population in Xieng Khouang, before, had goodness. And we built progress of good kind. And we helped each other to transplant and to harvest rice in the fields with happiness. But then came the time of change and it caused the people to go into the forests in the hills. We had to live in holes. We couldn't go out to see daylight. We had to stay in the forest as our home. One day the planes bombed the rice field of my village. And there was a young man about nineteen years of age who was hit.

—artist unknown

I am a child of my village. I once saw a horse of great size and goodness.
A man had ridden to his rice field and was hit by the airplanes. Only the
horse ran back to the village. We knew that this must mean the airplanes
had shot him. I went with the grownups to look for him. But he was already
dead in the field. When I saw this, I felt much pity for him. I saw his
children and wife and cried together with them. Everyone missed this man.

—a fourteen-year-old youth

Have pity on the victims
of the war!

a thirty-year-old woman

I am a woman. My name is Nang ——. Xieng Khouang has been my family's home since the time of my ancestors. But now it has been my lot to come to Vientiane province, the capital of Laos. I have in mind comparing these two regions of Laos here. For I know very well that there are big differences between them, and not only in economic development. There are also big differences in the two societies and the lives of the people; and in particular, in the life of one woman.

I was born thirty years ago, and I grew up with the benefit of the concern and guidance of my parents and began school during the period the government still occupied Xieng Khouang. By 1956–1957, I had grown into a maiden and had completed my primary school studies. And so it was that I fell in love with Thao —— and took him for my mate in 1959. But afterward I found that my premarriage days had been the only bright and happy period of my life. For after marrying, I found myself weighed down by suffering without end. My mate was a petty-minded and bad-tempered person, with many other bad character traits besides. During our courtship, he hid his weaknesses. But when we were living together, all of these bad traits of his began slowly to emerge. As for me, I was a person who thought in traditional ways. I believed that if one was born a woman, one had to endure all troubles until one's husband took pity so that his wife could be happy. I had never imagined that my husband would be as wicked as he was.

In 1960, I gave birth to my first child, a boy. But my husband was indifferent to me and went out with other young girls all the time. And that was not all. Mistreating me terribly, his parents took the part of their son and made me suffer. Feeling that I must endure all, and thinking of the future of my son, I continued to put up with it. In 1963–1964, the Pathet Lao occupied Xieng Khouang and established groups to teach the people in the various villages. They received women, older people, and those who didn't know how to read and write in the "schools of the people." And they took those women who were capable to be teachers or leaders of women's groups. They gave speeches saying that men were very wrong to believe that they were to rule the family, to believe themselves superior, to mistreat their wives, and to go looking for girlfriends without cause. After they spoke like this, my mate did not dare to act toward me as wickedly as he had. Then, because they knew that we still feared our husbands, because of our long-held customs, they asked me and encouraged me to stand up to my husband and not to let him mistreat and beat me. But I did not have the courage, and because of much housework or fear that he wouldn't be happy, I made up excuses to avoid the training courses that they were always giving. But in the end they won me over, for they would do things like bring friends over to look after me and bring me medicine when I was tired or ill, showing their concern or pity for me. Even when the war extended everywhere, they would keep in touch with me.

In truth, the life described above lacked a great many things, and it was very, very difficult to survive. For there was danger as the war came closer, like the sound of bombs or shells or the airplanes that constantly made a terrible noise in the sky and led me to be terribly, terribly afraid of dying. At that time, our lives became like those of animals desperately trying to escape their hunters. Our lives were confided to the Lord Buddha. No matter when, all we did was to pray to the Lord to save our lives. We didn't know how long we would stay alive. When looking at the faces of my children who were losing the so very precious happiness of childhood, as each and every day we would seek escape somewhere in the forest, I would grow increasingly miserable because of the war and hate it more and more.

Why then don't we people love one another? Why don't we live together in equality? Why don't we build happiness and progress together? To kill one another like this! Human beings whose parents brought them into the world and carefully raised them with overflowing love despite so many difficulties, these human beings would die from a single blast as explosions burst, lying still without moving again at all. And who then thinks of the blood, flesh, sweat, and strength of their parents, and who will have charity and pity for them? And then what about the splitting up of families to different parts of the country, which was caused by war? Who will pity them? In reality, whatever happens, it is only the innocent who suffer. And as for others, do they know all the unimaginable things happening in this war? Do they? Or is it rather that this war is something that benefits us and thus need not be stopped?

Last year through the efforts of the government—that is to say the national army—we escaped the flames of war. The government established us in the region of Vientiane, and aided us in our everyday lives. They have brought us to see this well-developed region, which has no war and where people lead their lives as they wish without all sorts of miseries. They have brought us out to see the sky and earth as other men.

But, on the other hand, there is much to regret; such as our houses, villages, and many other belongings, which have all been lost in the war. To come to this region is not like being in our village. Although our village is in the countryside, although it is small, we are accustomed to living there. It is not like here, where everything is already owned by others. We refugees who have come here are poor, and although their government has given us as much help as it can, we still feel a lack. It is normal that this should be so.

Those of us who are refugees here, we all think this way now: we pray that the war will end, that our parents and relatives and brothers and sisters who have been separated from us may all meet again, that we may again farm in happiness and live as we wish. That is all we want.

War causes a flood of blood. We don't need war! We need only peace! Let us help one another to build peace, oh human beings throughout the world! Have pity on the victims of the war!

My village stood on the edge of the road from Xieng Khouang to the Plain of Jars. There were rice fields next to the road. At first, the airplanes bombed the road, but not my village. At that time my life was filled with great happiness, for the mountains and forests were beautiful: land, water, and climate were suitable for us. And there were many homes in our little village. But that did not last long, because the airplanes came bombing my rice field until the bomb craters made farming impossible. And the village was hit and burned. And some relatives working in the fields came running out to the road to return to the village but the airplanes saw and shot them—killing these farmers in a most heart-rending manner. We heard their screams, but could not go to help them. When the airplanes left, we went out to help them, but they were already dead.

—*a thirteen-year-old youth*

In my village there was one place in the hills which gave the people a place to hide from anyone in the sky. But death did not flee us for long. Until it was hit by the airplanes shooting so that people died in the hole. There was no one who survived. They all burned and died. Only once in my life did I see many people die in hole like this. Because the airplanes mistakenly thought that it was a hole of the soldiers. So they shoot it up. But there weren't any soldiers who died. Only village people. Then in the days after that people went to dig out the bodies and recover the belongings which were of value. Everything was in the hole. The people who went to dig were afraid but they had to do it. Because their own families and children and wives, and parents were in the hole. There was one man who ran for the holes when he heard the sound of a plane but before he reached the hole he was shot by the plane and died outside the hole. His wife ran up but his heart had already given out and he had died. All that could be seen was blood coming out around his mouth. His bloody head didn't hide that day. And there was one old woman who ran up. She asked if anyone had seen her child. But all she saw was dead people. Her heart was fearful. She was afraid that her child had died already. She just stood there crying until she couldn't any longer. Truly there were people who died. Every, every day. They died because of the airplanes.

—a forty-nine-year-old farmer

Before, in the life of the rice farmers in this area, the village of my birth, there were wide fields and good earth and cool weather and mountains and forests, together in the life of the rice farmers of my village. This led to the building of progress and rice fields and harvests. In the first year of the airplanes we still went to thresh rice in the rice field. But the airplanes came and dropped bombs of napalm, burning our rice. It caused us to have no rice to eat.

—artist unknown

May the life of a former nurse
from Xieng Khouang pass away
without returning again

a twenty-six-year-old nurse

During 1967 and 1968, I was a nurse in Xieng Khouang. After having finished my three months of training and practical work with the Neo Lao health service, I was assigned to go around to the various villages, no matter whether near or far, carrying out as a matter of course my duties as the Neo Lao had designated. Because of my agreeableness and enthusiasm for my work, I won their confidence and also that of the farmers whom I taught and looked after. When I reflect on this, I can still remember very well my life as a nurse in Xieng Khouang, and so I will relate the story of what I experienced for more than two years. Let those of you who are interested listen, and learn something of me as well.

It must have been the spring of 1960. I was then a girl of sixteen and had never liked studying, not one bit, before then. I had no ideas about anything. I neither knew nor wondered how big or how little this world was. All that I saw and knew were a dozen or so houses in the middle of a forest. Around that village of mine were green and beautiful mountains, and the land and the fields my neighbors had sweated over and labored on since the time of my ancestors. My neighbors were all farmers, honest and hardworking. Our happiness was full and overflowing because we were content with our lives, even though we lived in the wilderness. We were sure that in this world very few people were satisfied with this sort of a life, that most people had only evil hearts that sought perpetually to enrich themselves without fulfillment. They were never content and all their lives had no happiness or joy at all. And so my life passed like that from when I was small until I was big.

I was at one with the earth, the air, the upland fields, the paddy, and the seedbeds of my village. Each day and night in the light of the moon, I and my friends from the village would wander, calling out and singing, through forest and field, amidst the cries of the birds. During the harvesting and planting season, we would sweat and labor together, under the sun and the rain, contending with poverty and miserable conditions, continuing the farmer's life, which has been the profession of our ancestors.

But in 1964 and 1965, I could feel the trembling of the earth and the shock from the sounds of arms exploding around my village. I began to hear the noise of airplanes, circling about in the heavens. One of them would stick its head down and, plunging earthward, let loose a loud roar, shocking the heart as light and smoke covered everything so that one could not see anything at all. Each day we would exchange news with the neighboring villagers of the bombings that had occurred: the damaged houses, the injured, and the dead; the graves dug for burial; the large and the small bomb craters. Each of these concerns entered and dwelt in the hearts of the people. They were exchanged for the age-old freshness of our village, which had disappeared completely.

The holes! The holes! During that time we needed holes to save our lives. We who were young took our sweat and our strength, which should have been spent raising food in the rice fields and forests to sustain our lives, and squandered it digging holes to protect ourselves. For many days and nights, having enough food to survive on became a gigantic problem that pressed upon our hearts. The fields, paddy, and seedbeds all became bomb craters. And many of our belongings were also lost from the war. All that remained for our people were sad faces, and tired and weak hearts, disgusted with hating the war, which was like a large stone weighing upon us. We could not understand or imagine why something like this could happen. When the bombing would diminish, we would seize the occasion to come out and rebuild our village, repair our homes, and continue farming to sustain our lives, so as to continue on as human beings.

Sometimes during this period, people called "cadres" entered our village, asking this and that. Sometimes they also went into the holes we had dug to escape the strafing and bombing of the airplanes. They displayed a kindly air and were interested in us. Sometimes when they saw us villagers building houses, growing vegetables and fruits, they would come and help us with the work. Over a long time we got to know one another. We would talk with them, finding little questions to ask them. When they saw we had questions, they were eager to answer us. When we didn't understand something, they would go over it until we did. Because of them, we learned many things that we had never seen or known. To choose an example: they told us that our village was no more than thirty kilometers from Xieng Khouang; if one walked on foot, it would take a full day to reach it. And they would tell us things about the city of Xieng Khouang, such as that it had a market in which people bought and sold things every day. This was not like in our village where we exchanged commodities. And sometimes they also showed free movies to the people. Many times we asked them to tell us about all these things that attracted us, and we wanted to go to the towns and learn about them as they had.

Later on, they asked those of us who were youths if we knew how to read and write. We said that we didn't. They asked, do you want to learn? We were surprised and curious. We asked them what letters were like. When they explained, it seemed to us that if we knew how to read and write, it would be a very good thing. We were attracted to the idea immediately and told them we wanted to learn. They replied that they were very happy to hear this.

Then they brought a very intelligent girl to live with us, who became our teacher and taught us to read and write. And when the villagers were sick, she had medicine to give them. She also went to farm the paddy and the fields with us. We saw that she was a truly good person. All the villagers also loved her very much. In the forest and in the paddy fields, she taught us songs to sing. For many days and nights afterward, we would sing. Wherever we were, whatever we did—although there might be the noise of guns, of planes, of shells—if we were together, the sound of the songs burst forth spontaneously. I can still remember one song that we sang:

The twilight is loveliest in the land of freedom.
Magnificent mountains, plateaus, forests, and plains
Mingle with the beautiful flowers giving off a perfumed scent.
All the nationalities,
With liberty and united in brotherhood,
Are fighting bravely to build a new life.
Dark clouds pass away; clear colors come instead over
The land so dearly beloved.
The blood of the fighters flows red everywhere,
Filling every nook,
Sacrificing itself in struggle to attack and vanquish the enemy.

This liberated region will be proudly guarded and its light extended,
Throughout the territory of Laos.

This was the song "Land of Freedom." Another song we liked to sing was called "New Life":

The new life fresh and shining
Like the moon, gives light
For happiness.
Suffering is like the wind that passes.
Having gained the new life, we will guard it.
The nation will be born again,
Growing in freshness,
And we will no longer see value in personal interests.
The filthy and evil life will disappear.
We will bring good and useful things everywhere,
So that these Laotian people will be happy forever.
This new life no one will ruin,
Because there is wise and clear guidance.
This new life we will gain
By the blood of the people, which colors all the land.
We must love one another.
Although the past life has been full of suffering,
Surpassing the strength of the people,
We will struggle against it worthily,
Blood and sweat flowing.
Let us guard Laos honorably,
Guard it for the great desire
Of the people who lead the land
Toward happiness and prosperity everlasting.
The new life no one will invade,
We will be joyous and happy forever.

Beyond this there were many more kinds of Lao dances in this style. Our life was transformed in the heat of the war and the joy of youth. After we had learned to read well enough for use, due to the influence and guidance of the Neo Lao and our own great dreams, we volunteered to study professions like the girl who came to live in our village. We wanted to be like her and have bright futures. And so, I, together with three of my friends, went to study in the town of Xieng Khouang. After a ceremony to say good-bye to our parents and fellow villagers, all four of us left for Xieng Khouang to search for a new life and new future.

When we arrived, each of us was satisfied. It was incomparable, as if the future we had dreamed of so long had become a reality. Then the welcoming committee took us to a hospital, where they had already prepared our living quarters. They made us feel at home although we were far from our village and families. After that, we took a rest. A few days later the hospital staff organized a welcoming ceremony for us. During the ceremony, various other friends who came from many villages in many areas assembled in one place, singing and dancing together after the president had delivered his speech. The president, that is to say, the hospital supervisor, expressed pleasure and happiness that we had the courage to come to study medicine for the welfare of the people. He congratulated us on our sentiments and urged us to study conscientiously so that our knowledge would increase and our work would advance smoothly. Thus the people would know and see that their children were preserving and improving their heritage without disappointing them in any way. This was the hospital staff's true goal, and he hoped that we would progress limitlessly.

After that night we began our studies. In the whole school we had more than thirty people. Studies were divided into two groups. One studied medicine; the other studied culture. The degree of our culture was low because we all came from the countryside; some students did not even know any letters of the alphabet yet. Besides studying, we spent our remaining time raising vegetables in the garden. Some people also raised ducks and chickens that they had brought with them. At that time the situation was just as tense, yet our lives were thoroughly well-ordered. We were told to live together and love one another: no matter when, no matter who, and if someone was ill, we were to take care of the person. Every Saturday an artistic evening was organized, and each of our groups would offer a presentation. We didn't get involved in other things or even think of anything else because we felt so satisfied.

Finally our studies were completed. After six months, we were capable of preventing diseases and treating other typical illnesses. We then went out to practice what we had learned, dividing ourselves up among various villages.

They had told us to eat and live together with the people. Our duty was to take care of the ill and act in such a way that people would believe and support the Neo Lao. At that time we did not have enough medical equipment, but the villagers expressed their need for us since few of the people in the countryside had ever received treatment like this. They had believed in spirits and had not been cured at all. In addition, we didn't take payments for our medical treatments. And so our work proceeded easily and well. Wherever we went, the farmers in the village would express the same love for us as they felt for their own children.

But a little while later, that is to say, during the years of 1968 and 1969, the situation became more dangerous, and we were not able to carry on our work as before. Every day and every night we sought ways of hiding from the danger from the air. Saving lives became more important than anything else. Our primary duty changed from treating diseases to helping find ways to protect the lives and belongings of the villagers. Nevertheless, there was work that arose whenever people were wounded by shells or bombs. For it was we who would take care of them and help them. Due to a lack of medical equipment, however, we constantly felt tired, weak, and anxious.

But then the situation changed, for soldiers of the government army entered the village where I was working. When they learned what I was doing, they took me with them under the pretext of pitying those of us living under the occupation of the Neo Lao. They also claimed that I was young and innocent and they would give me the chance to have a change of heart. They claimed to offer us protection and the chance to rebuild our lives in their villages in a new region.

And thus has my life passed. Were it not for the Neo Lao, I would have remained an innocent rustic in my village until I got old and died, and my village would not have enjoyed the benefits of any progress. And if the government had not taken us out, I would still be working ceaselessly for the Neo Lao.

Laos is progressing. Why then do some Laotians continue to fight and kill one another endlessly? Do they not realize how much suffering and poverty is experienced by the people, who are so sick to their stomachs with war? Who then thinks about their hearts? Who then will support them?

The past has melted away. Our lives have passed like a dream. There is nothing that can make up for the sorrow. The past is finished. Good-bye to old things. May the life of a former nurse from Xieng Khouang pass away without returning again.

My house and village were destroyed in the eleventh month of 1968.
Two F-4H planes flew over and bombed my village for forty-five minutes,
causing the destruction of many houses in my village. I was impoverished.
All of my belongings were burned, and I was caused great difficulties. Our
clothing was lost and we faced the future without hope and built small
shelters in the forest and jungle. But I had nothing with which to make a
living because everything was destroyed by the bombs. So I had to leave
my village with great sadness.

—a sixteen-year-old youth

Two years ago my life was 100,000 times more difficult than now because of the planes which came to bomb day and night as in this picture. We had to go dig holes in the sides of mountains or in the forest, so that we never saw the sunlight. And one day during this time, I myself heard the sound of the planes coming and I ran into the hole. Just as I reached the mouth of the hole, they bombed. I was so afraid that I would die.

—a twenty-six-year-old man

Before, my village had prosperity and good homes for Laotian rice farmers. This led to much progress for our wide land. But then came the present time, as we and our rice fields were hit by the planes and burned; our homes were hit and burned, our belongings completely lost. I think back and within me tears want to fall. But there are not enough. For I have fled from the village of my birth.

—*a twenty-one-year-old man*

Why did the planes
drop bombs on us?

a thirty-nine-year-old farmer

I am thirty-nine years old. My home is in Sene Noi Canton, Khun District, Xieng Khouang Province. I have been a farmer ever since I was able to do the work—for twenty-three years now. I have worked my parents' fields right up to the present. My parents accumulated many kinds of property, including paddy land, and various kinds of animals, pomelo trees, orange trees, large and small bamboo, and many other desirable things. I attempted to watch over and increase the holdings. It seemed as though we never wanted for anything in particular. Anything I wanted, I had. I had a dam to divert water to my fields for many years, and many neighboring families used that water. My paddy fields are wide, level, and regular. Surrounding the village is a wide field and steep mountain. And there are beautiful pine trees around the mountain, which can be used for house building.

Travel between villages was easy because there were so many villages all close together. Chatting with the girls at night or boys and girls playing the flute or the khene[1] and enjoying themselves in the village was easy. In the morning the girls would water the vegetable gardens and weave. In mid-morning they would go out to gather food along the creek, in the field, in the meadow—different people going anywhere they pleased. When it came time for the rocket festival, the young people would gather for the festivities according to our customs.[2] There were evening gatherings and happy, spirited singing repartee throughout the year, throughout the months—as

1. A mouth organ made of hollow bamboo reeds, about a yard in length.
2. The rocket festival (Boun Bang Fai) is one of the major holidays of the Buddhist-animist religion, which reigns in Laos. Its origin is believed to be a fertility rite, and its agricultural significance is that it occurs in May at the onset of the rainy season: the rockets being shot off into the sky to attract rain. The holiday is characterized by rocket

though we were fully content without a care in the world. At one festival a rocket competition was held by the edge of the village, with the drinking of whiskey and eating of chickens.

When it came time to work the fields, we went to work together. We shared the labor in a fulfilling way for us young people. When the field work was finished, we joined in the yearly festivities with the sounds of singing, dancing, and laughter. And there were the planting of fruit trees and the clearing of more land in order to accommodate the needs of the children being born. And my village also had a small market for buying and selling or trading, which made life even easier. The fields and meadows were filled with animals, and every house in the village had chickens, ducks, pigs, and dogs. My village was progressing steadily. The days of poverty were past. There were monks in the pagoda, which was very beautiful and decorated with different ancient pictures and carvings done by previous monks. The streets and roads connecting and running through each village were filled with the bustling activity of building our villages.

But then came a reversal of life for me and all the villagers in the canton. We had committed no crimes and had never said that we were going to do this or that. We had just built up what we had inherited. And because we hadn't had anything disturb us for many years, our building had progressed day by day. But starting in 1964, unrest reached my village. Every day we could hear the noise from big and little guns blasting continually. There were loud noises all over the mountains. It seemed as though our village was at the center of a storm shaking from great fear. But we thought these problems were no problem of ours. Our people would remain as before because we were neutral. So we prayed. Sometimes a shell from a large gun would fall in the village, but we thought it was just a stray.

But then all these things changed into something very different because war planes of the type T-28s and AD-6s, along with F-105s and four-engine planes and many kinds that I didn't recognize, flew through the sky over my village. They made a spectacle the likes of which my village had never seen. We came out of our houses and stood watching. In all our years, we had known no more than the word "airplane."

---

contests throughout Laos; individuals as well as villages compete to produce the most beautifully decorated rockets as well as those that will travel the farthest.

At first, these planes shot at the different mountains. We thought that our people had nothing to do with these matters; we thought we could watch to our heart's content and continue living as we always had.

But just then they started to shoot along the road to the village, which dismayed us because they were shooting without aim, and everyone became frightened and ran out to hide in the fields. At night we returned to the village and things continued as usual until March 14, 1967. Ours was the first village in the canton. Four planes of the jet type dropped their bombs together to destroy my village and returned to shoot twice in the same day. They dropped eight napalm bombs, the fire from which burned all my things, sixteen buildings along with all our possessions inside, as well as maiming our animals. Some people who didn't reach the jungle in time were struck and fell, dying most pitifully. By the time the fire died down, it was dark. Everyone came out of hiding to look at the ashes of the houses. Even the rice was all burnt. Everyone cried at once—loudly and agitatedly. Some families had been wounded. We were all heavyhearted and mournful almost to the point of losing our minds. The other villagers and I got together to consider this thing. We hadn't done anything, nor harmed anyone. We had raised our crops, celebrated the festivals, and maintained our homes for many years. Why did the planes drop bombs on us, impoverishing us this way?

Different people reacted differently. Tears flowed freely; there was no rice to put in our bellies. Then neighboring villagers came by the dozens to help care for the sick and wounded. They brought rice and helped us build shelters. Different people from the neighboring villages brought things to help us out. From a state of complete happiness, we had passed into misery and poverty.

As time passed, the planes came and bombed all the neighboring villages just as they had bombed us. Then the planes started viciously shooting in the forest and jungle and in all inhabited places, forcing us to steal away and hide in holes—to dig deep holes to live in. The fixing of food to eat together disappeared. The pagoda fell into disrepair; the monks were all hiding in holes and trenches. The miseries caused by the airplanes were immense because the bombs were large and if they fell in even a deep hole, everything would be destroyed.

These terrible conditions continued like this, off and on, until 1969. Then the Royal Lao Army came and took us to Vientiane for our own protection, but I didn't want to be separated from my homeland. When the time came to leave, I came away with many worries and concerns for the goods that escaped the fire. I was afraid and didn't know what I would find here. If the government doesn't care for us, they will surely see many deaths because building here is difficult. We don't have land on which to build, and we don't have animals like buffalo and things like in the past.

At that very instant when the gods were not generous, an event occurred that surpasses understanding, in which people lost their lives. This was another occasion of lakes of blood from the war planes' coming. These people were going together into the cave, but at that moment a bomb came without any knowledge of its having been dropped. This isn't like the courageous power of the skies in the time of Apollo; for this causes people to die without warning and in unknown numbers; some have their bodies completely blown apart.

—*artist unknown*

In the life of Lao people in which there was war, in a manner of which we are unable to say too much, it only happened this one time that I saw someone die in the forest in the hills. But wherever you went all you heard about was people who had died. There was one young man who died in the center of the forest. I don't know who he was. The time I saw him, there were just flies infesting him and crows eating the body. So that you couldn't tell who it was because he had died in the middle of the forest, four kilometers from the village. The family of one man had searched for him for many days but they never found him. That day after I saw the body, I went to tell that family about it so they could go collect the body. But they couldn't because it was already all decomposed. After that there was an eight year old child who was hit and wounded by the airplanes, but hadn't yet died. He just screamed in the road. Then the hand of an old woman led the wounded child into the forest for temporary shelter. Then when the planes had left she led him to a shelter where there was a hole.

—artist unknown

The day does not exist
when we will forget

a Laotian poet

Now I will tell you the story of times past. I will open my mouth and let my friends listen to the story I write here. Remember us; think of us before, when we were in Xieng Khouang. Awakening to recognize the morning, we entered the caves with the mice. In the evening we entered the burrows with the rats. If we hadn't escaped, we would still be in Xieng Khouang repairing the holes we hid in. The red ants and the black ants would crawl on us. It is our great fortune that the gods helped us. We would still be imprisoned in that embattled place if fortune had not brought us here. We used the jungle as our home. We used the moon and stars as our torches. We used the high branches to sit on and the low branches as our beds. We slept in the open by a big river.

Once we hid ourselves in the garden, digging some holes at the foot of the village. Then the planes went and demolished Sam Chong.[3] We left our village and went to live in Ton Thong for a month. Then we came back to our village. The planes went and beat Na Moun to dust. Boun Henang was killed in the yard near the clumps of bamboo. Grandmother was so shaken that she nearly died.

Fortunately we were hiding in the caves. We were very frightened. We went to hide at Phou Sa. We took our horses, cows, and water buffalo, but didn't let them graze. Then the soldiers came and repaired the camp near us so we moved from Phou Sa back to our village, where we built small shelters along both banks of the Nam Sene river. We dug holes on both river banks

---

3. This and the other village names that follow are villages through which the author passed in his odyssey.

with small huts arranged around them. The planes came and destroyed Ning Tom, the big village.

On foot we moved to Sene Muong, along the banks of the Nam Kho, making huts along both banks. The planes flattened Phou Sa. So we moved to Vang Khouai. The more days that passed, the sadder we became. We were reluctant when the soldiers told us to come and study about the struggle with them. We left home early in the morning, taking our lunches. After a while, we stopped and sat around in a circle. We paired off as a novice and teacher—each novice with his own teacher. After a talk they asked for rice and vegetables in order to support the struggle. When we returned home, we had to do the common work before our own work. We had to boil khao tom.[4] Even old people had to go and study with the teachers. The children went from door to door, collecting salted fish, red pepper, and tobacco. They asked for chickens and ducks. Also they asked for help in repairing damaged roads. Neither during the day nor at night did we rest.

As evening fell, the girls gathered flowers, which they made into wreaths and took to the camp. They wrapped the flowers around their arms, dancing, choosing partners, and forming a circle one behind the other. Singing, dancing the Phay Ngam,[5] some men playing drums, they carried on like this all night. Returning home, they said they had been husking rice. The old people had to dig up five or six seedbeds to grow manioc and sweet potatoes. Some girls manned the big guns in the camp. What a shock the bombing was, a cancer till death, causing heartache like a burning brand. At that time, we had to care for the children and couldn't prepare an offering to take to the temple. And the monks went into the forest and wrestled with logs in order to prepare upland fields for rice, which the monkeys came and ate. The monks worked without stopping to produce their share of rice for the struggle. Their yellow robes were unkempt and threadbare. They worked and hid in the jungle, their robes their only possessions. The novices grew weary. They left and there were no replacements. No flowers came to visit them.[6] Their robes were black, as though dyed with roots. Where once they used to carry their shoulder bags and go to meet with the "out women,"[7] now they

4. A sweetened rice and coconut mixture tied tightly in a banana leaf and boiled.
5. A distinctive Lao dance.
6. The laity would bring flowers to the pagodas as offerings.
7. Usually older women who have left the world to search for enlightenment in the Buddhist order; i.e., nuns.

hid in holes. We felt sorry for them. Prayer couldn't fill stomachs. The "out women" hid in holes in the jungle. No longer did they pray. No one could carry the small rice baskets to the temple and listen to the Buddhist teachings. Impoverished, our tears wet our pillows; we slept in the forest, curled on the ground with the grass like the snakes and evil serpents always hiding themselves in their holes.

We felt most sorry for the young mothers of newborn babies who couldn't sleep near the fire warming their backs.[8] If we made a fire, the planes would come. Day and night, we just worried without knowing what to do.

Many days small planes would fly over the houses. After flying over, they would call for the "black crows" [bombers] to strafe and bomb, ripping up the ground. Mountains became lakes where fish and crabs went to live and snakes and dragons swam and played. The planes show off their country's strength. The black crows are followed by the smaller planes and the spotter planes, which turn and watch without ceasing. The black crows drop bombs like streams of fire from the stratosphere. Hitting the ground, they burst into clouds of fire burning the land, houses, and paddies. Villages were blown into the sky leaving only pits for lakes and puddles where the fish and crabs would come to live, along with the dragons swimming and bathing in the chill waters.

Then we moved to Som Ngam. When we arrived, we dug holes under the tall grass where we could hide. These weren't yet good enough to live in when the small planes flew over. We dived into the holes; they were just big enough for our bodies. The spotter planes watched very closely. They were followed by the black crows, which came and destroyed everything, turning all into dust. That time we nearly died. So we moved from there to Vang Khouai. Some party workers came in the evening and told us to move to Muong Khoun. We implored them to let us stay until the next morning, when we would leave before lunch. When they had gone, we hurriedly ran back to this side. We went through the Sene Kang area where our old village had been. We went to Phou Thong Fa mountain where the Meo soldiers received us. They asked us about our situation and then urged us on faster. We traveled without resting, going through jungles and across mountains. Cross a creek, climb a hill. The sun burned fiercely. The sweat poured off.

8. After childbirth, a Lao mother traditionally sleeps over or near a bed of hot coals, drinking hot liquids and keeping to a very strict diet.

The sun was hot. The insects thick. We didn't have a lake to cool off in. We had only our labored breathing as we climbed the steep mountains, finally reaching a large camp where we rested. The Hmong soldiers gathered around us: "Fathers and mothers, you have arrived. You are fortunate. You have arrived safely. Welcome. Have all your people arrived? Your families? Or are some still imprisoned?"

We answered: "Many are still missing, Sir." Then the Hmong soldiers quickly brought rice, which was distributed to all of us.

After eating, I began to realize my poverty. Looking toward our village, we saw only dark clouds. Houses had burned like candles. Houses, rice fields, temples—reduced to dust. Smoke climbed the sky, darkening the country-side. And noises such as would frighten the gods. Even the dragons and ser-pents were scared. The black crows and jets had turned mountains into lakes, razed towns, and beaten the earth into powder. Now Muong Xieng Khoun was troubled, causing us to leave our village and town. What sorrow! We couldn't bring our cows, buffalo, horses, pigs, dogs, ducks, and chickens. We came away with only our bodies. What sorrow! Our household posses-sions in the houses waiting to be used were left behind. Pity our houses, rice fields, the places we built and repaired. Pity the flowers in the garden, which we used to pick and offer up to the Buddha along with bananas and sugar-cane. May the paddy fields along with the clumps of big and little bamboo fare well. Pity the lakes flowered with lotus blooms. The pools where we bathed are sad, and no one will come to play. Pity the fruit trees that we planted in the garden. May you fare well. Daylight comes, and we will go far away because of the foreign invasion of our country. We are separated from our village—the war has entered—and all we can do is to flee far away from the villages. I do not know where they will send us. Now we say good-bye to everything in Xieng Khouang. I will go to Vientiane.

We fled our village on the thirteenth. We reached the airport on the fif-teenth. We rested at Thamtamling for two days. Then the planes took us to Khoun Na. We were so poor. We asked for housing. How shameful to have to ask for a place to stay! After asking for housing, we built little shelters of grass and leaves where we could sleep with our children in the shade.

"Oh Soutta, my heart is heavy. My little boy, your mother has left you. We have been separated by fate—one of us to each side. You, my son, are with Souphanouvong. Your mother is on the side of Souvanna Phouma. Your mother has gone far away."

"Fortune has spared her, but she is so sad she does not see her fortune. My son, you lost first your father and then your mother. My heart, we are on two different roads with different sunshines. Bananas, sugarcane, tam som;[9] we cannot send them to each other. It is too much for my heart to bear, my precious little 'gold.'"

Now with tortured thoughts, tears wet our pillows. In our little huts, we listen. If anything blows by, it is sickness and fever. Many people die until there are almost no children left.

We left Khoun Na and moved to a spot on the edge of town. When we reached the spot at the edge of town, we built shelters on hard dry ground. There was no water for bathing. We were so poor for so long. We lack flavorful food. We went to catch fish, but the rivers and lakes have jealous owners and fines in the tens of thousands and hundreds of thousands of kip[10] have been established. Only at Muong Tcha can we gather food on public land without punishment. However, it was very deep so that our fishing baskets yielded nothing. We went to the jungle to look for food in the little creeks. We looked at the steep mountain cliffs. We wouldn't be able to get back down. We returned home picking leaves and catching a few fish. When we arrived, we bought some phak kat[11] for making soup. So flat! For we had fish sauce dip, salty sauce, and pepper. We had only appetizers for meals like pork rind. Take and suffer.

Listen to my story please: you ask me to fix my own lunch and supper. "Don't be sad, take your machete, spade, and make a garden." We made it good enough to get by. Then we went to catch fish, but when we go to get vegetables from the garden, they are still too young. We value them highly and want to save the seeds. We merely wasted our energy making these nice gardens from the seeds they gave us. After two months, it is taken from our mouths. Leave them for the army. Tomorrow morning they will take us away. It doesn't matter who the cattle and buffalo belong to; they will be shared. Too much! We built houses, but we haven't yet lived in them. We cry all night. Sorrow and hardship are our punishment. They visit us so many times. The time of departure has come. The village will become a stomping ground for the cattle and buffalo. Pity—our homes, rice fields, inheritance—we must abandon. The rice fields will grow jungles. They will become a wild place

9. A shredded papaya dish.
10. $1.00 = 500 kip (approximate 1970 equivalent).
11. A leafy vegetable like mustard greens.

filled with tigers. Have pity; the land, the ponds with fish, everything; pity the bathing hole where no one will come to swim and muddy the cool waters. Pity the crabs, fish, game, bamboo shoots; our kinds of food. Sorrow for the fruit trees we planted in the garden and around the village, the clumps of large and small bamboo; have pity! Daylight comes; the time to go, hurriedly away, far away. They will bring us together at Lat Sene tomorrow. Now we will say good-bye to the country of Xieng Die. The day does not exist when we will forget. Now I will say good-bye to Xieng Khouang.

In the year 1967, my village built small shelters in the forest and we had holes in the bamboo thicket on top of the hill. It was a place to which we could flee. But there were two brothers who went out to cut wood in the forest. The airplanes shot them and both brothers died. Their mother and father had just these two sons and were both in the same hole with me. I think with much pity about this old father and mother who were like crazy people because their children had died.

—an eighteen-year-old woman

Then they heard loud sound of guns so the three, father and children in one family, hurried forward searching to find a hole in which to flee from the falling bombs in the sky. But just then the bombs fell down on their heads before they could get into the holes. This and the lives of one family from my village in Xieng Khouang, they lost their lives in this way. Is there anyone who knows and sees the pity for and with them?

—artist unknown

Three jets came together dropping bombs

a sixty-nine-year-old former monk

I am sixty-nine years old and have always tried to live with a good and generous heart. This picture shows the pagoda in my village. I helped to build it when I was sixteen years old and a novice monk. When I later defrocked and left the pagoda, I still continued to help build it.[12] The construction of the pagoda was begun in 1916 and finished in 1930. It was in the center of Khang Canton, Muong Pek District, Xieng Khouang Province. It was quite big, with a large statue of the Lord Buddha and many novice monks. Every year we had many festivals in it. The happiness of the pagoda blessed and enlarged the school for teaching Pali, the language of the Buddha.

We always kept this old pagoda in good repair, even after the war of 1962, when it was partially damaged.

But then airplanes came to drop bombs on our village, at first just along the streets. So we could not gather in the pagoda because we were afraid to meet in the open that way. And thus we dug holes around the pagoda so that the women bringing food to the monks could be safe when the planes came to bomb. We also dug holes along the path from the village to the pagoda so we could have a place to hide when we brought food. This was the idea of the monks, who were very wise.

---

12. The priesthood in Laos is practiced quite differently than in the West, and indeed than in much of Asia. Most of the young men become monks, but most also defrock after periods ranging from a week to several years in order to marry and have children. It is customary for older men whose children are grown to return to the pagoda and spend their declining years as monks. Thus, for most Laotians, the priesthood is not seen as a permanent vocation, although there are a number of men who remain priests all their lives.

But even this was not enough when the fourth month of 1968 arrived. Among the planes passing over the pagoda, there was a small L-19 that spotted the monks taking their blankets to air in the sun in the yard. It remained over the pagoda, meanwhile calling in jets to come bomb it. Three jets came together dropping bombs. We gathered up some things and ran for the holes. Just as we reached the holes, the bombs exploded in the yard of the pagoda.

Right at that time two children were bringing food on a shoulder pole. They threw down their things and ran for the holes. They almost lost their lives because they were in a hole very close to the pagoda and the noise and smoke from the bombs went into their hole and made them sick and dizzy. The planes bombed the area until they saw that it was in flames; an hour and a half later they left. We tried to help the monks save some things from the pagoda, but the flames were too fierce. All we were able to do was to help the other monks out of their holes.

Thus we abandoned the pagoda of our religion, which we had been building and looking after for so many years. It was a great sadness for us. Afterward, we built a small pagoda in the forest where the monks could stay.

When we counted the holes left by the bombs dropped on the pagoda, we found that there were twenty-eight. And many bullets had hit it also. The pagoda was completely destroyed, all of it either completely burned or in ruins.

Everyone in the village had great sorrow for the pagoda, which we had cared for and honored for so many years. Afterward, we didn't know if we should build another pagoda. For we were afraid that if we did, it would be bombed also.

—artist unknown

Such is the life of the monks in the region of Xieng Khouang, a region of war. This truly I did see with my very own eyes: there was an old monk wounded and much blood flowed out, coloring his body red. For, one day he was in the pagoda, not having yet gone into the holes. And an airplane came and bombed and he was hit, along with a villager, who thought of and worried about this old monk. His elder came to pray over the old monk, whose death saddened the hearts of the villagers.

—*a twenty-two-year-old woman*

In my village there was a young man who went to graze his buffalo in the forest. The airplanes dropped bombs and killed the buffalo. The young man ran away from that place, but not in time. He was hit in the waist—cut right in half. For two days you could see him like that.

—*a twenty-two-year-old man*

In the region of Xieng Khouang there came to be a lake of blood and destruction. For there were airplanes and the sound of bombs throughout the sky and the hills. All we had were the holes. One day I saw a person who had been hit and injured lying near the mouth of the holes. But he couldn't get up so I went to help him and took him to the hospital. He was hit in the side so that he lost a lot of blood.

—a thirty-seven-year-old

These three were worried about their belongings. If everything burned up what were they to do in their future lives to have rice to put in their stomachs? These three, a mother and her two sons, ran out of the mouth of the cave they had taken refuge in. Their goal was to go into their burning home and retrieve some of their belongings for their future lives. But their fate was ended. For just then a bomb from the airplanes hit, a very big bomb. Though they tried to be careful, the fragments struck them. Thus all three people in this family lost their lives to the necessities of this war. This is the real fruit of war! That people die for no reason and no result.

—*artist unknown*

There was an old woman who went to the village to get rice for her children and family to eat in their holes. But that day the planes bombed and she died apart from her family.

—*artist unknown*

He and his wife died together in the rice fields because of the airplanes

a twenty-two-year-old woman

Xieng Khouang is a region rich with mountains, forests, many upland and paddy rice fields, and a fresh climate. Lao people have lived here for many years. They are all farmers, all Laotians. But it is not developed as other places are, for in this land there is nothing but war, which has caused us Laotians to fall into misery and poverty. Always thinking of the past, I am unable to forget this place. And because of this, I will tell the story of what has passed in its life, and what caused changes in the life of its people.

I remember that back in 1957, the government here in Vientiane still ruled in Xieng Khouang. During that time the people were happy, because there was no war. We did not use different kinds of machines and things, because we were farmers. My family and fellow farmers had long been in the region, living by the strength of our hands. It did not matter to us that there were no machines or factories. We farmed upland and paddy rice to sustain ourselves for all of our lives, although it was to be our destiny that a certain time would come to turn our lives upside down.

In 1958 there was a good deal of commerce, with most of the goods coming from Vientiane, although we grew our own food and rice. Every Lao person grew upland and paddy rice and farmed vegetables. There were only a few people who did not have any rice fields to farm.

But in addition to the good things, there were also many bad ones: There were no factories or machines; houses were not modern but built in the old style. Some people had many rice fields and would hire people to farm for them. Most of the rich thought only of making profits and tried to entice the farmers to abandon their fields and become workers or sharecroppers for them. In 1957 and 1958 foreigners, such as rich Chinese merchants, got together with high-ranking officials in order to import goods to sell from Vientiane. Seeing many goods coming in, those who thought wrongly went along with this kind of society, and many people were led to abandon their rice fields, gardening, and orchards.

In these years there were also many people who smoked opium because the hospital was far from the villages. Secondly, they did not have the money to afford to stay in the hospitals. Some people that I have known went to stay in the hospital one or two months, and then returned home without any money to pay back the doctors. So they had to kill buffalo or cows to pay them back, and thus would not be able to farm their rice. I saw many examples of this kind of situation: There were thieves, liars, lazy people, and those who made women become whores. People were allowed to become addicted to gambling and the lottery, and when they came back home, they would beat their wives and children; some people would become divorced because of this. Nor did women have equal privileges with men.

In 1960, Kong Le liberated Xieng Khouang and then changed our lives somewhat. That is to say, it was almost the same, but there were slight changes. The important thing was that one didn't have to pay taxes and could live as one pleased. The Kong Le party also increased the number of hospitals. Above all, in agriculture, they encouraged the farmers to produce. They built roads, built up the town of Khang Khay, and installed electricity through-out the towns of Khang Khay and Xieng Khouang. There were many, many vehicles coming and going, and it was not necessary to spend money on carfare. There had been vehicles before, but one had to pay to ride, and one had to rent houses. But at this time we saw that things improved. Goods came from many places. At that time one could move freely all over the Plain of Jars and Xieng Khouang. Old people, young people, and boys and girls rejoiced in making festivals and ceremonies, and many people went to the pagoda. But this was not really different at all from before.

In the fourth month of 1963, our lives were changed again, as danger came to the Lao people of Xieng Khouang region.

The Kong Le and Neo Lao Haksat parties split apart once more. It became difficult to go from Xieng Khouang to Khang Khay, as the two sides did not agree with one another. The Plain of Jars region, Muong Soui, and Muong Khoun were occupied by the Kong Le party; Xieng Khouang, Khang Khay, and Phonsavan were occupied by the Neo Lao party. At that time the people dispersed everywhere. Some people left to be with the Kong Le party, but the majority remained in the villages of their birth. For they didn't want to abandon the rice fields, cows, and buffalo that they had cultivated for so many years.

In 1964 the Kong Le party left the Plain of Jars, and the Neo Lao Haksat introduced a new style of administration with a new economic, educational, medical, and social system.

As a young girl, I had found that the past had not been very good, for men had mistreated and made fun of women as the weaker sex. But after the Neo Lao party began to administer the region, if one makes a serious comparison, it became very, very different.

On the subject of women: under the Neo Lao, things changed psychologically, such as their teaching us that women should be as brave as men. For example, although I had gone to school before, my elders had advised me not to. They had said that it would not be useful for me as I could not hope to be a high-ranking official after graduation, that only the children of the elite or rich could expect that.

But the Neo Lao said that women should have the same education as men, and they gave us equal privileges and did not allow anyone to make fun of us. Women could also work. For example, I helped my parents plow and grow vegetables just the same as the men did. And they did not let husbands divorce their wives. But what I liked most was that they didn't let people be prostitutes, thieves, liars, or idle. For the Neo Lao party taught these people to be good people, like the rest of us. Before, there had been beggars and poor people, but now there were none. They encouraged husbands and wives to love one another; and women would do men's work and men would do women's work, each helping the other willingly. For to my knowledge, in my village husbands and wives did not disagree with each other as they had before. The Neo Lao had made men and women equal.

And the old associations were changed into new ones. For example, most of the new teachers and doctors trained were women. And they changed the lives of the very poor as well with their new systems. For they shared the land of those who had many rice fields with those who had none.

For example, there was an old couple who had no children. Before the Neo Lao came, they were beggars, took opium, and had no house to live in. In 1965 we all helped them to build a house and to grow rice because we pitied them for being unable to do it themselves. Afterward, the doctor took the old man to stay in the hospital for four months to cure him of his opium addiction. When he returned, he felt very happy.

He told us that before he had had a son. When he was about forty-five, the old man had been taken ill and was hospitalized. After about six months, he was still not completely well. In the end, the old man had to kill four cows and buffalo to pay the doctor. But even this did not bring enough money to pay the hospital, so he had to send his son off to work for the French to get the money. But as a result, the officials drafted his son into the army. The old man never learned what had happened to his son; he just lost him. Later, he had to become a beggar to get enough to eat. He had a rice field, but couldn't farm it because he wasn't strong enough. For he never was completely cured of his illness. He had to take opium to feel better and thus had become addicted. But in 1966 he began a new life, for the farmers changed their old ways of thinking in this new era. Because of that, they helped the old man build a house, farm rice, and finally, succeed. He didn't have to go hungry, nor beg like before. Nor was he ill any longer. He felt terribly happy although he regretted one thing. If he had changed his life more quickly than this, he would not have had to lose his son.

This story was a lesson to us. For everyone knew the story of the old man who had been a beggar but who now had changed and had happiness like other people. This is the truth; I saw it with my own eyes.

But it was terribly, terribly sad. For one day, jet planes bombed and cost him his life. He and his wife died together in the rice fields because of the airplanes. I wept very much, miserable over the loss of his life. If he had not died, he would have come out with us.

The old man was about fifty-three, and his wife was forty-eight. His house was quite close to Route 7 in Canton Khay, and his house was at the foot of Phou San. He lost his life in September 1968.

Now I will tell you the story of my past. When I lived in my village, it was difficult for me to study because I was a woman, and I endured much hardship. During the period when I went to school, I tried my best, although I was only a simple villager from the countryside. But I could go to school only part-time, having to help my parents as well as study, for I was the oldest child in our home.

My school was located next to the household of the canton chief. It was a very small school. I went to study there in 1957. There were more boys than girls in this school, about forty boys to only six girls. This was because girls were mostly not allowed the privilege of studying at that time. As a result I decided that I would have to study.

After I had studied for about four years, the Kong Le side attacked and occupied my village. Because of that I had to stop studying for about two years, until the Pathet Lao liberated my village. About six months after that, the village and canton chiefs decided it would be good if I went to study in Khang Khay to learn to be a teacher in the "schools of the people"; that is, to learn to teach older people how to read and write. And so I studied in Khang Khay for a year and a half. Before, studies had been conducted in foreign languages, like French, but I felt that I learned more studying in the Laotian language for a year and a half with the Pathet Lao than I had learned before in three years. Also, I didn't have any family problems during my studies at Khang Khay, because our neighbors helped my family with the farming as they wanted to have me study to be a teacher. I was happy because when I went to study this time, I found my studies easy, because I didn't have to learn in French as in the old system. In this new system, we learned only in the Laotian language. After I graduated, I returned to my village, and after a vacation of fifteen days, a friend who was my assistant and I established a group of about eighteen older men, and another group of about twenty-four older women. My assistant was a man, and he taught the older women. I taught the men. At first, I found it terribly difficult to teach, for there was no schoolhouse. But we would study at home, or sometimes we would go to farm rice together and study while we rested.

In 1968, however, studies became even more difficult, for airplanes bombed my village a great deal, and also bombed in the forest around it. But I forced myself to summon up the enthusiasm to teach, to help these people learn, because they had worked so hard at their studies already. If we abandoned our studies, it would deprive the people of knowledge. But in 1969 it became impossible to teach. We could not go out of the holes, as the airplanes bombed near my village every day. They bombed our villages, homes, and rice fields so much that we didn't know what belonged to whom any more. Before my village had had a large forest, but now it was completely gone. Only the bare red earth was left.

But what is important is that although I am in Vientiane, and I am living well, I cannot stop thinking of my old village. The climate there is fresh and healthy. When I think of the past, I cannot sleep. If it were not for the airplanes that bombed us, I would never have left. If there were no war, it would be a joyous event in my life.

Thus I have spoken of my thoughts of the past.

This village woman was a person of good character. She spoke softly and sweetly and never gave sorrow to any person for any reason. Why did she have to die so pitifully? She died in the middle of the forest beside the cow she tended. She died in misfortune with unsurpassed sadness. The outlaws in the airplanes did this, bringing fear to our country such as we had never before seen. The airplanes truly killed the people at a time when we knew nothing about what was going on. They came to do this, why? When you see this, how do you feel about your own brothers and sisters and relatives? Would you not be angry and concerned? Compare our hearts to yours. And what are we to do?

—*artist unknown*

One friend of mine went to the village to get rice for his mother and father to eat. He crossed the field to the hill and the airplanes saw him and shot and killed him so that you couldn't even see his body. It was scattered all over the field.

—a twelve-year-old boy

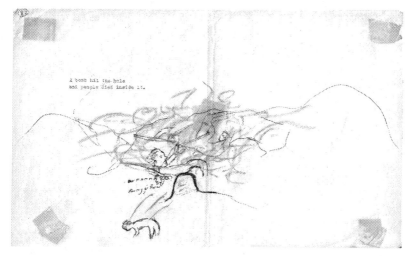

A bomb hit the hole and people died inside it.

—*artist unknown*

And so we sang with brave hearts

a fourteen-year-old boy

When the situation changed, I had to leave the place of my birth where I had lived all my life. I remember my native village with much sadness because it is a generous region that provided me with a comfortable life while I was growing up. The land, sky, and air are cool and moist, giving one a feeling of pleasure and satisfaction. And so, I think of the time when I worked in the paddy and gathered food in the forest nearby. For me, there is no place to compare with it. The mountains and forests are filled with so many useful kinds of birds and animals. Neither paddy farming nor building homes was difficult, for all the villagers would help one another with the work, and it was extremely gay and happy for us young people. That place, though it was very rural, and composed only of forests and fields, was perfect for me.

And we would respect our customs in our pagodas. Boys and girls and older people would observe our usual ceremonies and holidays.

But then the airplanes came and bombed our dearly beloved land, causing us to lose our cows, buffalo, and fields in a grievous manner.

But my friends and I did not fear the airplanes' menace.

We also learned a song that the Pathet Lao had composed.

This song was written by the air-defense soldiers of the Neo Lao. But we learned it anyway. We loved to sing it together in the rice fields during the rainy season. We would sing this song gaily, and it would encourage the young women and make them happy in their work until they finished.

I felt that although I might have to die, it did not matter; that I just had to be happy in the midst of all the sadness of war, of the airplanes dropping bombs till the sky was filled with the sounds of the planes or the fire of the anti-aircraft guns.

And so we sang with brave hearts.

The following song, which we often sang, was entitled "The Air-Defense Song."

The Air-Defense Song

Let us praise the air-defense batteries who have the bravery to fire at
　　the American airplanes invading our Laotian skies.
Flying here they appear and are shot down and destroyed by our
　　air-defense positions.
Let us harken to the sounds of the guns echoing all day, as our
　　air-defense batteries fire until the Americans disappear.
Come F-105s and T-28s; we will fire at you until you are destroyed.

This song was written in 1966. And it makes me think of my sad, sad past. For the climate is hot here in Vientiane, and earning a livelihood is difficult. I am not used to the climate. I do not have the training to work as a civil servant. And so I long for my village.

I have made up my mind. No matter what, whatever happens, I must return to my own land.

Then the F-105 warplanes strafed and dropped rockets and 150 kg bombs on the village and people without stopping

a twenty-eight-year-old man

This picture shows the airplanes bombing the town of Phonsavan in the year of 1969, the month of July, around Wednesday the thirteenth: There were F-105 airplanes that attacked my village from 6 p.m. for one hour. These airplanes flew around in the sky, passing back and forth. At one time there was an L-19 that dropped a smoke bomb on the village in order to mark the place for further bombing. Then the F-105 warplanes strafed and dropped rockets and 150 kg bombs on the village and people without stopping.

So the people's houses burned and were completely destroyed. The people were hit by bombs and killed, and more than thirty were wounded.

Because these airplanes dropped bombs on the village without stopping, the people had no place to go to escape. They had never before experienced anything like this. It caused parents to be taken in death from their children and children to be taken in death from their parents in great numbers, causing the people's tears to flow. Because the airplanes had dropped bombs on the rice fields and rice paddies, the people saw that they could not withstand these hardships. So they fled into the forest and the jungle or different streams and caves.

We saw that it wouldn't end, so we fled to the side of the government of Prince Souvanna Phouma, the prime minister. Because the war was so severe, we had to flee from our homes, rice fields, rice paddies, cows, and buffalo and come here in poverty.

This picture is in 1967 when the T-28 planes destroyed the houses of the people. In December 1967 around the 5th, the airplanes destroyed the homes of the people. Many planes dropped many different kinds of bombs: poison fish K-ME, rockets, 150 kg bombs, and anti-personnel bombs. This caused great destruction for the population, killing and wounding more than 40 people. At the same time, T-28's attacked the village almost constantly from 12 o'clock until 6 o'clock in the evening. After that the people were most afraid and troubled. Never before had they experienced war conducted by airplanes with so many people losing their lives or being wounded in consequence. The people who lost their lives were those hit by the anti-personnel bombs or the 150 kg bombs or by the rockets. In this picture I have depicted the 150 kg bombs, or rockets, and anti-personnel bombs. At the same time the bombs struck the people's houses, destroying all of them, causing fire as well. This caused great poverty for the people and shortages of many kinds. After that the war grew worse every day until it was impossible for the people to lead normal lives and they fled into the forest and jungle to hide. Then in 1969 the people saw the poverty, suffering, and oppression they had withstood. They saw that they couldn't withstand the bombing by T-28's. So they fled from their birthplace, Muong Non, leaving their rice fields, paddies, cows and buffalo until the present time.

—artist unknown

A bomb fell about fifteen meters from where my father was plowing

a sixteen-year-old student

I will tell about my past life in Xieng Khouang, an area with high mountains and scattered open plains. It is naturally beautiful because the climate is cool and misty. In the mornings, fog shrouds the mountain. In the evenings, the rays of the sun silhouette the mountain in a most charming scene. And turning, you can see the water cascading from the top of a high mountain.

I lived in Xieng Khouang in Canton Boon, Muong Khoun District, Xieng Khouang Province. My village was near a large mountain cliff face. In the evenings, I like to climb the mountain up to the cliff, taking along a cap and ball rifle as a friend.

I am only sixteen years old, and still a student. I helped my parents with the field work as much as I could. I helped with the progress of my household, as should be the case with a child who is loved. There was no one else in the house besides my sister and me, so I had to help my parents in the field.

My older sister didn't have a chance to study—only I studied. I started school when I was seven. I did well each year, and my classmates liked me because I was not a troublemaker. My family had enough food and clothing. I went to study in the morning. In the evening, I came back. Then I would round up the cattle and buffalo and put them in the pen on the tall mountain. There was nothing to worry about because everything in my region had always been the same.

When harvest time came, my paddy yielded a good deal of rice, which was threshed and stored with great delight. Since I lived near the school, it was easy for me to help my parents and sister. I enjoyed my village's natural setting. There was a river running past the village making fishing a simple

matter. I didn't have to spend money for anything because we could find
enough of everything right in the village, except for clothing, which we
bought. I often looked at the pine trees above my village. In the village itself
there were six houses.

But in 1964 a strange and different thing disrupted the tranquil life I have
described. T-28s and jets began to fly over my village every day, making a
terrible racket, constantly startling me, and making me afraid. I had never
known anything like this in all my life. But my father was a person who was
not afraid, and he went about working the fields and gardens as he pleased.

One day the noise of a bomb indicated that the planes had started to shoot
along the road. Turning to look, we saw that they were bombing the large
town. I was very frightened, but continued on as usual. Every day I went to
school. But then some planes bombed a neighboring village, Ban Het Hai,
on the edge of the forest. The village was completely burnt down, and many
people and animals died. Everyone around me squirmed with fear. The children didn't want to go to school because the teacher planned the digging of
a hole near the school. Study in the morning—dig in the afternoon. When
the hole was finished, we continued to go to school as usual.

After that the planes came all the time, making life very difficult. Wherever you looked, the planes bombed, destroying fences, fields, gardens, storage bins, and houses. Life became very difficult for everyone. You couldn't
light a fire to cook food because a plane would see the smoke and bomb it.
I became ill and also felt sad because the school had been closed since the
schoolyard had been completely destroyed. My sister and I tried to dig a hole
deep enough to ensure that we would escape with our lives. Later, I got better and school reopened but with only a limited time to study. When the
sun was high up in the sky, we had to stay in the holes. But my father was a
very diligent and industrious person and persevered in his work. When the
planes came, he would hide behind a paddy dike. When they had passed,
he would come out. He did like that all the time as the planes continued to
come angrily, day and night.

At night they dropped flares in search of a place to bomb; if they saw
people, they would fire at them. During that time, we had to leave the village
and fix a little shelter at the foot of the cliff. Under these conditions, I was
afraid of becoming sick because my heart was so very sad. The place where
I used to play on the mountain and the place where I used to bring the cattle
and buffalo in the evening to shut them up had become so many bomb

craters. And I couldn't go into the woods anymore because they had been sown with antipersonnel bombs—some hadn't yet exploded. Sometimes an animal would kick one, and it would blow up. Consequently, we could come and go along only a single narrow path. If you left the path just a little ways, there was a good chance of your stepping on an antipersonnel bomb! During that time I merely husked rice and returned to the hole in the gully in the jungle. But my father felt sorry for his animals. He slept in the village and tried to plow early in the morning. He was afraid we would all die of starvation in the coming year if he didn't farm. When the sun came up, he would retire to a hole.

But one day my father was plowing when, unexpectedly, the fog shrouding the mountain all disappeared suddenly. In no time at all, a plane flew over, but it appeared as though it wouldn't fire. My father stood in the field with the buffalo watching for the plane to pass so he could unhitch the buffalo. But suddenly four planes of the F-4H type flew over and immediately released their bombs. The bombs destroyed my village. All six houses burnt, and a bomb fell about fifteen meters from where my father was plowing, causing the blown-up earth and the shrapnel to kill my father and the buffalo instantly. I didn't know what had happened to my father because I hadn't seen it. I was in the deep hole far off in the gully. When the planes had gone, I was afraid my father might have been hurt and came out with my sister. We stared toward the village, full of fear. Then we went into the village and saw all the houses burning and the animals dying in the fire. Then I saw my father lying with the buffalo in the plowed earth. My sister and I ran over to him, but I saw that my father was already dead. I wept, and then I carried him out of the field.

Then we went to get the villagers to help take care of his body. When father's body had been cared for, the planes came again. They dropped large flares at night and saturated the area with small gun sweeps. Because of that, I was at my wits' end. Our possessions were all gone. I had only my life left.

In 1969 the Royal Lao Army soldiers came and brought me here to Vientiane. I am completely unhappy because I am very homesick. I remember being able to find my own food and shelter as I pleased. But here, though the government cares for and looks after my family, I can't build anything because everything belongs to the government. If I want to plant a garden, there isn't any place to do it. If I go to look for a place to live and for food to eat, for fish from the lake or stream and for water to use, the people here are jealous and do not let me use them, so I must go hungry. Every day I have to buy food for breakfast and for supper, and now I have no money left. What am I supposed to do? I am very sad, though at least I can come and go without fear of the planes. If the government someday has land where I can build, I won't be so unhappy because I will be able to earn my own living. I have done it before. If I have enough paddy land or a house, some place to live, it will be enough. Maybe I won't go back to my old village. I can survive on very little because I have withstood poverty for many years already. I just want to see peace, happiness, and progress before the end of my life.

This is the end of the story of my past life.

In the area of Xieng Khouang, the place of my birth, there was health, good earth, and fine weather. But then the airplanes came, bombing the rice fields and the forests, making us leave our land and rice fields with great sadness. One day a plane came bombing my rice field as well as the village. I had gone very early to harrow the field. I thought, "I am only a village rice farmer, the airplane will not shoot me." But that day truly it did shoot me and wounded me together with my buffalo, which was the source of a hundred thousand loves and a hundred thousand worries for me.

—*a thirty-three-year-old man*

There was a woman who had only one son, whom she loved most dearly. He never cried and her heart was always happy with her child at all times. But one day the airplanes came and gave her heart unhappiness, for her son was struck by the airplanes and his leg was broken and his arm hit. It made him cry so, a cause for much sorrow. All children born into this world have hardship, but not like this.

—*a nineteen-year-old youth*

Then they bombed our village; hitting houses, the pagoda, the school; devastating our rice fields; and killing the cows and buffalo

a seventeen-year-old boy

The village in which I was born, so pleasing to me, had a cool, fresh climate and rich mountains and forests. There was also much land for rice fields and raising livestock. For many years, I raised cows and buffalo, as my parents had taught me to do. I saw this as very beneficial and enjoyable for someone living in the countryside, for a farmer who inhabited the mountains and the forests.

Thus in the year 1959 I was looking after cattle in my village, together with others, working to help my family. My village was near the Nam Ngum River and bordered the mountain Phou Khout. It had long been prosperous. It was flat, as well, and in some places there were pine forests. Each day I went to look after the cows and buffalo. Having gotten up and eaten, I would pack rice to take with me, and go out together with four friends. My household once had had only a dozen or so head of cows and buffalo. But then they had reproduced themselves until we had more than fifty head that rarely got sick. That made me feel happy, and I was happy to tend them. I was enthusiastic, for I found the work of raising cattle in the forest really enjoyable. Each day I had to go out early, and in the evening I would return home. Then I would work some more, helping my parents with their plowing. At that time, I was not studying in school, for my rice fields were far from the village. Each year the rice grew very handsomely in our fields, and I felt great pleasure when the rice was ripe and yellow. My house had surplus rice every year. Sometimes, my mother took rice to sell in the market, but this was most difficult to do because there were no roads, only small trails through the forest. That is to say, at one time there was no progress in that region. Because of that, one had to leave my house at 3 a.m. in order to reach the market by 6 a.m. The market was held near the town of Phonsavan, close to the Plain of Jars airfield, once every five days. Most of the goods we sold were only what could be grown, such as all sorts of fruits and vegetables, ducks and chickens. All that we would buy was clothing. As for other things, such as foodstuffs, we could make them ourselves.

Schools were only in places where a great many people lived. There was no school in my village. To go to school, it was necessary to leave in the morning, taking rice along, because it was so far away. As a result, children in the six-year-old category could not go to school; only those over ten could go. And thus almost no one went to school, and everyone followed in the path of the old traditions. As for me, I did not study well, sometimes going and sometimes not.

In 1961 Kong Le's party liberated my village. But there were no changes, nothing to be afraid of, and everyone lived as they always had. But at that time my household had to sell pigs to the soldiers of Kong Le because there was no money to buy opium. My father had smoked opium for a long time, since the days of Phoumi. For at that time there were no hospitals nearby. When my father became ill, there was no one to cure him, and the only thing he could do was to smoke opium to feel better. One had to have money to go to the hospital, and it was very far away.

After Kong Le entered my village, his followers built a school. Many people went to it because it was so near, including my friends and me. But I did not have much enthusiasm for learning because I missed the animals I had been looking after. When I went to study, my parents looked after the animals. In the evening I would return home and go out to look for the cows and buffalo to bring them back home.

In the third month of 1965, the Kong Le army left my village when the Neo Lao party liberated it. Because of that, the students had to stop school again, since our teacher had left with the Kong Le party. We had never seen the Neo Lao party at all, and everyone was afraid, and ran to hide in the forest. The government party had told us that the Neo Lao party was used to eating people, and that whatever village they entered, they would also take the cows and buffalo of the people to eat. They said that if we didn't allow them to do that, the Neo Lao would kill us. Because of that we chased our buffalo and cows into the forest. We were also afraid of the big guns over at Muong Soui. This all made it difficult for everyone, and we were all afraid of dying.

After a while, I saw the Pathet Lao chasing the people out of the forest. We were afraid but felt we had to listen to them, and so we came out to live in our villages. They didn't allow us to farm rice as usual, but they didn't kill us or take things from us. Some people were afraid, mostly those with money. They offered cows to the Pathet Lao soldiers to eat, but the soldiers refused to take them. If they did take them, they paid a suitable price. The truth is that they led the people not to be afraid of anything.

Then they organized the election of village and canton chief, and the people were the ones who chose them. But they prevented the election of a person who had repressed the people in the past. Then they established youth associations, women's associations, and "cooperation groups." In whatever work that was done, we would help each other. They didn't let people be poor as before. Everyone had to help one another. As I saw it, they changed things like this. And they changed politics also, having everyone study politics. And they built schools to teach in a new way, not allowing the old way to continue. They put a big emphasis on the Lao alphabet. In the old days, there were only about ten students, only older ones. In the time of Kong Le, there were thirty students, big and little. In the time of the Pathet Lao, there were forty-two students, big and little. And in addition, they established "schools of the people," to enable the older men and women to study reading and writing and politics. In the beginning, some people liked to learn and some did not. Afterward, when they saw that those who studied really did learn to read and write, everyone wanted to study. In the old days, the French language was held higher than Laotian. In the time of the Pathet Lao, only the study of the Lao language was allowed.

But because the war was unending, it was difficult for the people in that region. Farming was not as easy as before. Because my village was between Muong Soui and the Plain of Jars, artillery shells would fall on it, killing some of my cows and buffalo. During 1967 and 1968, airplanes came to bomb our mountains and forests. Then they bombed our village; hitting houses, the pagoda, the school; devastating our rice fields; and killing the cows and buffalo. It was horrible. At the same time our rice fields were 60 percent lost and not a single house remained. They bombed for three days, without letup.

Then we went to live in the forest again because there were no houses left in the village and it was impossible to live in the holes we had dug within the village. For when the airplanes had already bombed some place, we were terribly afraid to remain there. In my village, an entire family died in a hole from the bombs. But when we went to live in the forest, the airplanes also bombed there, suspecting that there were Vietnamese soldiers there. But there weren't. The result was that two more children died because of the bombs, because they didn't get into a hole in time. Many belongings were also lost.

Life for us was terribly difficult in this region. People were struck in the forest and in their villages. We didn't see that the planes actually bombed any soldiers. If they did, we didn't hear about it. And the airplanes also dropped one kind of poison I know of, which made cows and buffalo die, because it was dropped in the forest and the animals didn't know what it was. They would go to eat the poisoned grass, then return home to die. Sometimes, we saw it drop in the water or on the rice fields: pigs, ducks, and chickens would also die because of it.

Afterward, in the ninth month of 1968, we all left our village to live about six kilometers away near the foot of a large mountain in a very large forest. We built very small shelters and dug holes in which to live together. But when the rainy season came, the holes became muddy, and little children and old people would die because of the mud and because they never got any sunshine. Cows and buffalo also died in the village; they were bombed by the airplanes until none remained. Very few animals were not struck, and we didn't know where they had run off to. I was terribly sad and miserable because the buffalo and cows I had taken care of for so many years were all killed. Because of this war, I had to lose my cows and buffalo, village, home, and rice fields.

And in addition, many villagers died. Afterward, when I was about to come here, I went to look at my village, and I saw only the bones of cows and buffalo.

In the ninth month of 1969, the government side attacked and occupied our area. Then they called us to get into airplanes to go to Long Tieng. As for me, I did not want to leave at all. But I had to because my home, cows, and buffalo no longer existed. And thus it was that I and my neighbors left our old village.

Since I have come to live in Vientiane, the only good thing has been that we are not afraid of airplanes; nothing else.

If there were no war, truly I would not want to be here. Although the government occupies itself with us somewhat, I still miss my upland fields, my rice fields, the mountains, and the forest. Although my region is in the countryside and not developed, that does not matter to me, for it is the place that nurtured me and has been the home of my ancestors long gone, a place once full of pagodas and prosperity, with a fresh and pleasant climate.

Since I have come to Vientiane, I have been sick often, because the weather is hot and does not agree with me. Many children have died of diseases. And also, there is no wood with which to build houses, and we do not have any real homes. If the war ever ends, I will return to my village that very day. And if there is no plane to take me, I will walk all the way.

In my life I once saw a person die like this. One day we had already gone into the holes, but there were some people who had been some place else and didn't learn in time that the planes were coming to bomb. One man was hit in the stomach and his intestines came out, together with much blood. It was very frightening. One man went out to help him, but when he got out there and saw what had happened he was afraid and didn't have the courage to go any farther. He told me this since we are from the same village.

—*a sixteen-year-old youth*

In my village we raised rice to earn our livelihoods as we had always done among the mountains and forest with prosperity. But this prosperity was destroyed by the dreadful craters of the bombs from the airplanes throughout the region. Not only this but there were also many kinds of poison. There were the bombs of napalm which would burn houses and people. And there was a kind like a leaf. And there was the paper which would blow in the wind. If anyone would pick it up they would be like the person in the picture. There were many kinds which would kill people. We were most afraid of these things. If we went anywhere we had to be most careful.

—*artist unknown*

I will explain about this kind of poison which I know about and which
I saw. This kind of poison was in long, long lines. The planes dropped it on
the forests and in the hills. If it was dropped on the rice field and touched
the rice, the rice would die. A person who picked it up would become very
hot. And if it fell on people who didn't know what it was, they would die.
Many people, most of them children aged eight or ten years, didn't know.

—*a thirty-seven-year-old man*

In the year 1968, planes of many kinds and many types came and killed people. In the war in Xieng Khouang I saw the poison in the packets like candy. We villagers and children didn't know if this candy from xxx could be gathered and eaten. But after eating it people became drunk and threw up blood and died. We didn't know which day we would die. Everyone just waited for the day of their death. All day and all night the airplanes never stopped bombing. And they dropped poison and napalm in the village and in the forest wherever the villagers stayed.

—*a forty-two-year-old woman*

We lived in holes all the time

a fifty-one-year-old farmer

I am a Lao. I am now fifty-one years old. The village where I was born and bred is Nalông Noi, Kheung Canton, Muong Pak District, Xieng Khouang Province. My old village was beautiful and bountiful enough for my needs. I had a wooden house with a grass roof. All around were mountains and beautiful fields. Beside the village ran the Nam Ngum River. I am a man who prefers the traditional ways of life and work: planting trees, digging fish ponds. Ever since I can remember, of all the things my parents led me in, I preferred building over all other means to prosperity. Nothing could shake my determination to progress by building. The climate of my village was pleasantly cool, constantly shrouded in fog. During the rice season, we all went together to work in the fields. During the gardening time, we made gardens. It was my desire to build even more than I thought was possible for me to do. I had a beautiful house and eighty to ninety animals: buffalo, cattle, and horses; around the village and in the fields were large numbers of the different small animals. I lived comfortably and was pleased and happy with my good fortune, for I provided for all my needs and never had to ask anyone for anything. I had many paddies and produced much rice every year. In my family there were thirteen people—each one happy and content because the area was so bountiful and beautiful. In the evening one could see the animals returning to their pens in a great unbroken herd after a day of searching for grass. When I would see that, I would feel content because these animals were my heart. If I needed money, I could sell them or some of my other property.

Speaking of festivals, I participated in "Kong hôte"[13] with much cheer— from the rocket festival through all the others, respecting them according to

13. Ceremony acknowledging a higher level of attainment by a Buddhist monk.

the Lao customs. There would be as many as seven to eight hundred people attending, the boys and girls joking, playing, and drinking whiskey together, making merry in every home. These festivals were held after the rice had been harvested and stored. There would be five or six of them every year.

The building of the temple was begun as a never-ending task. I felt very happy doing such work as transplanting, house raising, gardening, threshing, and carrying manure or performing other kinds of work that required helping each other—or what we refer to as working in a way that never knew tiredness, that produced results no matter what the project, and that never worked anyone in excess of the person's strength. We shared the work in our village until almost no one ever had to spend money to hire someone. Thus was demonstrated what farmers who love one another can do. The trees I had planted were green and pretty around the village. Trees bearing both sweet and sour fruits, when ripe, provided fruit for the others as well as for me. In my village, many people had nice houses, and some people increased the size of their fields year by year until the eighth month of 1962.

I became distressed because the peace that my village had known for so long passed into war. I had never known anything like the noise of the big guns dropping shells nearby. I was frightened and didn't dare to farm or gather food. Then I grew used to it and forced myself to work for fear of hunger. In 1963 the shelling increased, but life was still livable because it was only the big guns. However, it caused many animal deaths. I still persisted in leading the family in working the fields and paddies, amidst the noise from the guns. When the noise grew too loud, we would take shelter behind the paddy dikes. But we still didn't forget our former life. The festivals and the sharing of work had greatly decreased, and the amount of building, farming, and planting had correspondingly decreased because of the difficulties involved. In 1964 and 1965, airplanes came dropping bombs on military posts, on roads, on bridges, and on the different towns. The countryside, like my village, fared better with less passing back and forth, but we had no respite from fear. We stayed in the village and never went to visit our relatives. I still worked the fields as usual, thinking that the planes would shoot at the military posts and camps, in the mountains, and along the roads as previously. Our provisions were reduced by only one-third. In my village, six homes had been burnt as a result of the planes strafing and bombs exploding, so we dug holes away from the village and always slept in them during that time. But the intensity of the bombings increased. Day and night, the bombs dropped in profusion, filling the sky with smoke from the explosions, shrouding the entire canton in shadows. Wherever I looked, I would see the smoke rising out fantastically from every neighboring village. It seemed as though there were many wounded; and no one would come out to rescue things from the houses or help extinguish the fires, for one might be hit by the bombs and gunfire from the planes. Everyone was ashen—as though without blood from fear and anguish over their lost possessions and animals. I myself stood in a deep narrow hole to escape death. Things had reached the point that in order to farm, I had to dig holes next to my paddy fields. When the planes came, I would immediately jump into a hole. Sometimes when walking from one place to another, I would break off a tree branch with many leaves and carry it so that the planes wouldn't see me. Food production had decreased drastically along with the gathering of food. We ate rice with nothing else, making us weak. We knew that in the near future we would surely lack even rice and our animals would die. We had only the ground for a home. Poverty became our lot as our piles of stored rice or the newly ripening crops were depleted.

During the three years, 1967 to 1969, the bombing was very intense. The planes fired at the village more frequently. My home was hit by a gasoline bomb [napalm] and completely burned down, while the bamboo I had planted around the house was smashed and broken. The field was hit by a large bomb and destroyed. Five houses and upland and paddy fields were destroyed, and five cattle were killed. I was very dispirited, for now I didn't even have a house. I endured these hardships; I slept in the trees and built a small hut. But it still wasn't over. Even more planes flew overhead, day and night, causing us great fear. We dug a hole and built the hut over the hole. When the planes came, we dropped into the hole. Sometimes we didn't eat. When bombs would drop near the hole, the ground would shake and my tears would well up. At such times I would think, Will it end or not? I have led a good life. I have laid up much merit. Surely this will come to my aid. With such thoughts, life went on.

When sadness and depression settled over me, I didn't want to build anything or do anything because I was afraid everything would just be destroyed again by the bombs. Where I had once known happiness and gaiety, now I knew only sadness. We couldn't go anywhere. Wake in the morning; stick your head out of the hole; if you hear a noise, dive back into the hole. We had been forced to abandon our gardens and fields. We couldn't work for fear of the planes. I put all my strength into digging holes in four different places.

I tried to make my holes deep. We lived in holes all the time. During that time, any gaiety or visiting ceased; all was quiet. Want and poverty increased from day to day as my desire to act stopped, causing greater shortages of rice, water, and even fish.

This continued until January 8, 1969, when soldiers from the Royal Lao Army captured the Plain of Jars. They brought us to Vientiane where it is safe and nothing will harm us and life is healthful. I very much didn't want to come because I miss my former village so. I miss the cattle, buffalo, and other animals. But because of my great fear of the never-ending gunfire, I decided to leave my fields and gardens, the various animals, and all my fruit trees and bring only my body here. But when the plane took off and I looked down at my village, I was immediately so homesick for my village, my birthplace, for the region where I had lived my life day by day.

I came away with sorrow for the animals I had cared for every day. Now, who would look after them?

When I thought of these things, the tears flowed profusely, pitiably, until I reached Vientiane. The government listened and processed me very quickly, which put me at ease. But now all the land here is theirs. If I start to make paddy or cut upland fields or gardens, there are owners who claim possession. Thus I while away my time without any place to build. If in the future, the government will grant me some land, I will build, make paddies, and support myself. But if in the distant future I should have good fortune, it will be to return to my birthplace.

But then came the time when the airplanes came and destroyed all our homes. And though we had to work to rebuild our rice fields, we had to go live in the hills and forests so that we never saw the sun and our children turned yellow. The most difficult time for me occurred when I was living in one big hole with many other villagers and one day airplanes dropped smoke bombs on our hole, causing us to become dizzy and throw up blood so that we couldn't run away. People screamed for their relatives or anyone else who heard to come and help. This is how it happened in my canton.

—*a thirty-eight-year-old man*

In earlier times my village had good fortune and there was nothing to cause us fear or danger in our region, as all over Laos. But in 1965 the airplanes began to drop bombs on the people of Xieng Khouang, and caused deaths and injuries. As in this picture, there were people who died in the holes. Many people couldn't get out. All that could be seen were heads, and legs, and hands. Then there was a man who went to dig them out because his wife and child were buried inside.

—a thirty-two-year-old man

These two, father and son, don't have hands and feet on account of a bomb dropped by the airplanes that didn't explode right away. They thought it would never explode and went to pick it up to look at. It exploded, hitting them as shown in this picture. Now they can't do anything. But this father and son pair did not come away with us. The father said that he would not go anywhere even if he was killed for it, because he regretted the loss of his land, rice fields, cows, and buffalo. Even though they couldn't work, they could still look. So they refused to come, and they said that it was because of having been hit by the bomb. Leaving wasn't any good. Better to die in the village. This was the decision of these two, father and son.

—*a twenty-four-year-old man*

All we saw was the fire of the firebombs everywhere. One day I saw the planes come and I ran out with my child. But my child's skin was hit. I took him and ran for the forest. There were some other people who tried to take their belongings and run out of the houses with their children also. But the houses were old and big. They were hit by the airplanes and burned and we were not courageous enough to go back and get any more of our things. After that day I always stayed in the holes in the forest, for I didn't have any house at all. I made a very small shelter in which to stay.

—*a thirty-two-year-old man*

My village was destroyed completely until it was level. The fruit trees were all knocked down, completely lost.

—artist unknown

In the forest, I would go
from one hiding place to another

a thirty-nine-year-old rice farmer

Why was it necessary for refugees to leave their native villages that had nurtured them for so many years? Let me tell you of my life.

I was born in Canton Kang Sene. My village had vast rice fields, stretching from the north of our village farther than the eye could see. My house was situated next to the rice fields. My family were rice farmers by profession and lived on the rice harvested from our fields each year. We didn't buy any rice from others to eat. Since always, I farmed rice to feed my family, and would have been content to do so forever. My village was in the countryside, amidst a large forest with a cool and pleasant climate. Our rice fields were also large and handsome. It was not necessary to use fertilizer because the rice fields were surrounded by forest, and the leaves that fell made a rich and good fertilizer. As I would look at the rice in my field every day, I would feel content that it was growing so well. I would also grow our vegetables and fruits, for my house had a very lovely and fertile garden. Each year I would feel very happy. I grew rice faster than my friends did, and in my garden would raise such things as peaches, bananas, sugar cane. I had about ten trees of each. They gave good yields of fruit, and I would give them to my wife to sell in the market in Xieng Khouang, since at that time, the country was still at peace.

Our government party still occupied the area, and some things were easy at this time. In my opinion, this was primarily because there was no war, and commerce was also easy. But my village was deep in the forest, and cars could not reach it. Because of that, we traveled by horse when going on long journeys. But most of my family and neighbors did not need to buy many things. The important thing was material for making clothing. Food—rice, meat, ducks, chickens, and fish—we produced ourselves. We would help each other make houses by cutting down trees, sawing wood, and building. Cooperation in my village was based on mutual aid. When doing anything, we would help each other, as if we were all relatives. But education during that period was not all that easy to come by because there were only a few schools for those who lived in the towns. Although some cantons did have one-room schoolhouses, I couldn't send my children to study at ours because it was too far away for them to go and come easily. And then in that period, as was the tradition, it was not necessary to study in order to eat.

But I felt that if there were a school nearby, I would send my children to study. In 1958 I went to dig in the mines at Ban Mon. I was a coolie for the French big men in order to earn money. But after sixteen days, I got sick and returned home. I couldn't farm that year because I was so sick. There were relatives who came to help, but it wasn't the same as when I did it myself.

The most miserable thing about my village was that there was no medicine or hospitals. Because of this, when I was ill, I had to go to the hospital in Ban Ban, Muong Kham, about ninety kilometers from my village. I had to sleep in the hospital because it was so far away from my home. My wife could not bring my rice to me because there was no one to look after the cows, buffalo, and garden or to take care of our children. So I slept in the hospital for two months, spending 40,000 kip. At that time there was no development as there is today in health or education.

Our most enjoyable pastimes during that period were the ceremonies in the pagoda. And helping each other harvest during the rice-harvesting season made my heart joyous, as the boys and girls would sing and dance in the rice fields. At that time we didn't know death, and I never dreamed I would be evacuated to come here.

In 1965, the Neo Lao party liberated my village. During the battle, some people fled to various places, but I decided that I would never leave my home no matter what. If I ran away, I would not be able to farm and would not have any rice to eat, and my cows and buffalo would destroy my garden. Afterward, there were tremendous changes in the methods of farming and in education and politics. Life was tremendously different, although things went on as usual in the domain of observing religious ceremonies. Farming also went on as usual, without restrictions. Before there had been card-playing and the lottery and opium-smoking and beggars in the towns. Now, even in the countryside, even the poorest had enough upland and paddy rice fields to grow food to eat. And not only did the Neo Lao party make these changes in the old society, but they also had us change our old ways of thinking.

When they came, they established various organizations and associations. And there was one school for my village, with a teacher from our village itself, to which I sent my children. They established both a primary school and a school for older people, and so I went to continue my studies at night. During the day I farmed together with the other farmers, growing rice and vegetables and leading our lives as usual. I raised pigs, ducks, and chickens and sold them at the cooperative or else to the other villagers. That is to say our life in the country became self-sufficient, and unlike before, products came to us from Vientiane or big merchants. After 1965 and 1966 there were no big merchants, and whoever wanted to buy goods bought them at the cooperative or else took rice to exchange for cloth or blankets. At that time everyone did much farming, and I could not sell my fruits and vegetables as before when just a few people farmed.

But our life became most miserable in 1965. Airplanes came and dropped bombs on the road and in the forest and mountains. I had to go and dig holes deep in the forest. Our life was not comfortable as in the past, because of the airplanes' bombing. When they first came, they didn't bomb the villages or the pagodas. Although we were afraid, we still farmed and went to market. At this time we could also dig holes near the villages. We didn't need to go far to escape.

But one day in 1966 I was plowing my rice field at eight in the morning. Four airplanes came and bombed our village's pagoda, which was a forest pagoda. Returning home on that day, I saw that the pagoda was destroyed although, just by luck, nobody had been killed. From that day on I was terribly afraid, and the village and district chiefs told us to dig our holes in the forest. I went to dig a hole about two kilometers away from my village. I had the children sleep in the hole, and I returned to guard my house. If I heard an airplane overhead, I would run to a hole.

During the eighth month of 1967, airplanes bombed my village. Just at that time I was on my way to bring rice to my wife and children in the forest. If I hadn't already left, I probably would have been killed in my home. On that day, my belongings were lost, and my house completely burned down: nothing remained. Our pigs, ducks, and chickens also ran away into the forest, and I looked but could not find them because they were afraid.

From then on, the planes bombed every day. After they bombed my village, they bombed the roads and the small paths, and also completely destroyed our rice fields. After that we had to dig other holes even farther away because we were so afraid. On the days that the airplanes would come, we were so afraid we didn't want to eat. I pitied my children, for when the airplanes came to bomb my rice fields, they were afraid and afterward would weep loudly. I was very afraid and could not even close my eyes to sleep.

In 1968, there were no houses remaining in my village at all; and all my cows and buffalo had been killed. As I had no buffalo to farm with, I had to borrow some from my neighbors. Previously, I had gone farming early every year. After my buffalo died, I had to wait for my relatives to finish plowing and then borrow their buffalo to plow my own field. As I farmed, I tempted fate in exchange for my life. For, if I didn't farm, there would be no food to give my children. Hiding in the forest, I would go from one hiding place to another. We dug holes until there were no more places to dig. My fear led me to believe that life could not continue.

In the first month of 1969, the planes bombed more than we could bear, so we took refuge in Phonsavan, living under the care of the district chief of the Neo Lao party. We couldn't farm in our village. Thus we lived there for one month until there was no rice to eat there also, and then returned to our village. But once there, the airplanes came to bomb each and every day and night so that we couldn't leave our holes at all.

Two months later, the government party attacked my village, and the Neo Lao fled. At that time my relatives left with the Pathet Lao, and I came on the government side to Long Tieng. But each time I think of the past, I want to return to my village. I am sad that my house, rice fields, and buffalo were lost. If the airplanes had not bombed my village, my house would not be lost, my cows and buffalo would not be lost, and I would not have left. Even had they threatened to kill me, I would never have agreed to go.

But because I did not have a house to live in and had no cows and buffalo, I was forced to leave the village of my birth in order to survive. If someday the country is at peace, I must return. If there is no airplane to take me, then I will go back on foot.

—artist unknown

My village was hit often by anti-personnel bombs and other bombs from airplanes. My house was hit and I lost everything. I knew the war and was very afraid, but I could not flee. At that time there were small airplanes which shot bullets down where we slept. I ran away to seek my friends in the forest but as soon as I ran out, they shot up my house.

—*a twenty-two-year-old male teacher*

They died like animals die in the forest

a twenty-seven-year-old man

1. My village used to have hills, forests, and homes next to our rice
   fields.[14] Everyone had rice fields, buffalo, and cows. We earned our
   livelihoods with happy hearts. We always helped each other to
   develop our upland and paddy rice fields. But then came the airplanes
   to strike at our houses until they were completely lost, until we had
   no place left to live. And we were afraid because the planes came
   almost every day. It was as if we were in jail. We couldn't go anywhere.
   All we could do was sit in the mouths of the holes.

14. The narrative of the picture goes from right to left.

2. And still there were people who were killed in the forest and in the rice fields every single day. At least once every day you heard of someone being killed. We would put them in a box in order to take them to be buried in the forest.

3. In the third phase, we couldn't even put them in boxes anymore because we had no more wood. We just dug a hole at the foot of the hill and buried them. This is how it was when the people died in this region. They died like animals die in the forest because the planes bombed every day. Therefore, we were afraid and didn't have the courage to do the right thing. Someone died, and we just took and dumped the person and ran back very fast. Some people were not even buried; they were just dumped in a box and left in the forest.

A life whose only value was death. I saw this in the village of my birth, as every day and every night the planes came to drop bombs on us. We lived in holes to protect our lives. There were bombs of many kinds, as in this picture I have drawn. It is not beautiful but it shows the shooting and death from the planes, and the destruction of the bombs. This kind of bomb would explode in the air and was much more dangerous than other ones. I saw my cousin die in the field of death. My heart was most disturbed and my voice called out loudly as I ran to the houses. Thus, I saw life and death for the people on account of the war of many airplanes in the region of Xieng Khouang. Until there were no houses at all. And the cows and buffalo were dead. Until everything was leveled and you could see only the red, red ground. I think of this time and still I am afraid.

—*a thirty-three-year-old woman*

This is my house, built of lumber twenty-six years ago. It was struck by the airplanes.

a forty-nine-year-old farmer

1. I am forty-nine years old.[15] This is my house, built of lumber twenty-six years ago. It was struck by the airplanes that dropped antipersonnel bombs, causing everything to burn. It was very early, and we didn't have time to take things out of the house, so everything was lost on October 3, 1968.
2. The Kot stream, which flowed past my house, was very beautiful.

---

15. All the numbered items and incidents in the text are pictured (but not numbered) in the drawing.

3. My rice field was at the mouth of this stream, and I went with my buffalo to plow the rice field very, very early in the morning.

4. During the day, someone from the house brought food to me in the rice field. Right then I heard the sound of airplanes coming, so I ran away from my buffalo. I didn't have time to unhitch it. I had only the paddy dike to shield me while the planes shot and burned the village. When the airplanes disappeared over the hills and I raised my head, I was greatly upset to see the house and storage bin burning along with the hills and forest nearby. So I ran to look in my hole, fearing that someone was injured. After running a little way, I saw that bombs had fallen along the road and then saw my younger sister who had come out to bring food to me. She had thrown down the food in order to flee into the jungle, but she hadn't escaped. A bomb hit her there on the path, causing severe wounds. When I reached her, I couldn't take her anywhere because the planes turned around overhead in order to make another pass. I had to drag her into the forest and then slip with her through the forest to a hole to escape the fire from the planes.

5. This is my nineteen-year-old sister. She had stopped to pick some vegetables but just then the airplanes came, and she had nowhere near to run to. So she ran for the jungle, but was hit by a bomb first. She lost a limb and thereafter was unable to work.

6. This tunnel was drilled into a tall mountain about three hundred meters from the village. It had two entrance holes and was about fifteen meters deep. In order to make it good protection against the bombs, we dug for a very long time, at least a month and a half to complete the hole.

7. Shelter for the buffalo to sleep at night.

8. Tôh trees and orange trees grown for their edible fruit.

9. A 500 kg bomb fell on top of the hill in back of the village, covering the area with black smoke.

10. One antipersonnel bomb canister released not less than three hundred bombs, which fell all over, killing and wounding many animals.

11. Hit by a bomb, the forest above my hole burned.

12. Fear caused the buffalo to run away. Some animals died, and smaller animals like pigs, chickens, and ducks also fled or were killed.

During that time I thought of my house and belongings, and everyone in the house had to wash away his or her tears. Not a day would go by that we would not get up and go into the holes. We would stay in them every day, all day long, taking only what we could carry into the jungle and forest. We didn't have even a little happiness. Difficulty and deprivation came every day. The rice was nearly gone in less than a year because of the fires from the bombs. These difficulties enveloped my heart. So it was until 1969 when government soldiers seized this area. I came away with many worries. When I arrived here in Vientiane, the government assisted and provided for me so I wasn't completely depressed. But if the war ends, I will return and rebuild my village.

One time in the year of 1967, my old aunt carried things to sell in the market as was her old custom in the countryside. That day she arose at six in the morning, put fruit into her basket and then walked out of the village on her way. Just as she arrived at a place where there was a small stream, she stopped to rest. An airplane saw her and shot a smoke bomb at her. She was afraid and then as she sat there her body was hit. Blood came out everywhere. She decided to run and just as she arrived at the house she died, before she could say any last words. Her children and her husband were most angry that they had lost her so. Everyone was disconsolate. After that day no one ever went to the market anymore.

—*artist unknown*

This hole was dug in 1968. It was in a hill so that it was hidden from the sky. But before long there was an airplane which dropped bombs on the hole. It killed everyone in the hole. There were many people whom you couldn't see at all. Only two could be seen. Of one all you could see was his head and of the other all you could see was half of his body. Most died inside the hole. Everything was leveled. I saw this and was sent to help dig the people out. But digging was most difficult because the hole was full of bodies. There was one old man about 58 years old who heard that a hole in the village had been hit by the planes and therefore he was very disturbed and most afraid because his wife and child were in that same hole.

—artist unknown

Epilogue

After the War Ended,
1975–Present

When the war ended in 1975, the people of the Plain of Jars achieved their wish. They were allowed to return to the land of their birth. But they found that land deeply scarred by war. Their homes were destroyed. The thousands of water buffaloes they had once used to plow their fields were gone. They lacked food, often existing only on emergency handouts of rice. They lacked money, tools, almost all of the rudiments of life.

But by far the worst problem they encountered as they tried to plow their fields, catch fish, or pick bamboo shoots and other plants in the forest, was the unexploded cluster bombs from the bombing that still littered the earth. These cluster munitions would often explode, claiming life and limbs. Even after the war had ended, the cluster bombs and other unexploded ordnance continued to kill or maim some 20,000 Laotian peasants. In addition, the prevalence of cluster bombs everywhere deprived the people of the Plain of much land they badly needed to farm because of the cluster bomb danger.

Meanwhile, U.S. leaders who had spent more than 70 billion in today's dollars bombing Laos did little to clean up the estimated 80 million unexploded cluster bombs they left behind. Only an estimated 0.28 percent of the land contaminated by unexploded ordnance has been cleared although the bombing stopped in 1975. The bombing has thus caused immense suffering to the villagers of Laos for the past thirty-five years, and will continue to do so for the foreseeable future.

In May 1993, twenty-four years after the motorcycle ride that brought me to the refugees and thereby changed the course of my life, I returned to visit the Plain of Jars.

I found the land filled with energy. Everywhere I looked, from the capital town of Phonesavan to dozens of villages, to mountainsides, I now saw people building, scurrying, going to and from the market, hoeing the land, tending their cattle, praying at the pagoda, partying. The marketplace was jammed with people from a dozen different tribes. In Phonesavan there was a copy shop where you could get photos and Xerox copies made during the four-hour-a-day period when the generator was running. Many villages had television. The bad news was that soap operas, tawdry game shows, and insipid musicals had finally reached the children of the Plain of Jars. But the Plain was still a place where the children gathered around you, followed you through the village, and then, when they got to the pond, stripped off their clothes and dove in, joining you again a few minutes later, refreshed.

My old friend Ngeun was alive. But the land was filled with ghosts.

As we drove about for four days, Ngeun and our guide would talk, softly, as Laotians do. "What about Nang Sao's father? Where is he?" Ngeun would ask.

"Killed back in 1967, walking down the road," the guide would say.

"Oh," Ngeun would respond and then sigh, remembering some detail of the man's life or character.

We visited Ngeun's cousin, a sad man of perhaps fifty, with many children. A farmer, he now lived in a large house by a dusty road in the small village where Ngeun's wife had grown up prior to coming to Vientiane. It was an open Lao-style house on stilts; only the stilts were not very high off the ground, and the wood had a rough-hewn, cheap feel to it, unlike the deep dark rich wood—as smooth as only wood could be that had been walked on by bare feet for decades—that was found in traditional Lao homes before the war.

How many head of cattle did he have today? I wanted to know.

"Eight," the cousin said.

"Great!" I said.

"Not so great," he explained. "We had a hundred head in 1965." I realized that Ngeun's cousin and families like his would farm ceaselessly for the rest of their lives and still not be as well-off in 2010 or 2020 as they were in the early 1960s.

Then in November 2010 I returned to the Plain of Jars following the First Meeting of States Parties to the Convention on Cluster Munitions (CCM) in Vientiane. This international treaty, first enforced in August of that year, prohibits further use of cluster munitions, provides assistance to the victims, and promotes clearance of contaminated areas and destruction of stockpiles. At the meeting in Vientiane, the parties to the Convention adopted an action plan to ensure effective and timely implementation of the CCM's provisions.

Forty-one years had elapsed since I first discovered the bombing in September 1969, and Vientiane was palpably growing, with the mixed blessings such growth entails. Money, it seemed, was pouring into this country. Chinese, Vietnamese, and Western investments in gold, timber, and other raw materials were revitalizing its economy. A high-speed rail line was to be built in the next five years between Laos and China. And then there were the hydroelectric plants. "Laos will be the battery of Southeast Asia," a high-ranking Lao official had told me years earlier, and now I heard it everywhere. But some believed that development might come at a high environmental and human cost. Many nongovernmental organizations voiced fears that the growing industry would force Laotians to relocate to where it would be harder to develop sustainable livelihoods and that dams could threaten the ecology of the Mekong itself.

In Vientiane there were whole new neighborhoods that hadn't existed two years earlier and traffic jams at peak times of day. Motorbikes were everywhere. I remembered how, years ago, I had effortlessly tooled around a tiny, leafy Vientiane on my motorcycle. The idea of a traffic jam in those days was unimaginable.

Yet up on the Plain, the effects of the bombing were visible everywhere. Hundreds of bomb craters were discernible from the air. I discovered one even in a meadow above the lodge where I was staying, and remnants of the bombs were ubiquitous, as many people used the metal from them for the walls and roofs of their buildings, for receptacles to hold water, and for many other purposes.

And the cluster bombs are still killing and wounding many people every year. Most of the people living on the Plain are still subsistence-level farmers, and still have far fewer water buffalo with which to plow their fields than they did fifty years ago. Many of the cluster bomb explosions that still kill and wound people occur because people are so desperately poor that they are forced to go out into the uncleared forest to search for fish and vegetables for their families, or to risk their lives looking for bombs, in the hope of selling them to the Vietnamese traders who buy them for a few pennies and then sell them as scrap metal to local foundries.

On Day 3 of the conference, news reached us that a ten-year-old girl named Pui had been killed and her fifteen-year-old sister, Paeng, seriously wounded in her knees, body, and neck after Pui had picked up and then thrown away a cluster bomb in central Laos. The *Vientiane Times* had published a photo of Pui's corpse. The visual and story gave those of us at the conference a sense of added urgency.

Though the Lao government did a fine job managing the conference, which was a great success, it was unclear how much additional money would be garnered to actually clean up land contaminated by cluster bombs. The Swiss government, for example, announced a donation of $5 million. Yet given the fact that in the last forty years Laos has cleared only 0.28 percent of its contaminated land, such sums were clearly not enough. To make any real progress, many more tens of millions would be needed, and hundreds of millions of dollars would be required to clear the land entirely.

At the conference, the United States was never mentioned. It was as if the bombs had just magically appeared, with no one responsible. The U.S. Embassy refused to attend the conference as an "official observer." They sent only a low-ranking official, who distributed a statement boasting of the $50 million the U.S. had contributed since 1975, failing to note that these funds had cleared but a tiny portion of the unexploded bombs the U.S. had left behind. The United States, Israel, Russia, and other major users of cluster bombs had neither signed nor ratified the treaty. The Lao government, wishing to pursue closer relations with the United States, did not venture a critique. Great Britain had ratified the treaty but was clearly protective of interests. Weeks after the conference, a WikiLeaks document revealed how Britain had conspired to violate the treaty by stockpiling cluster bombs for the Untied States.[1]

On my last night in Vientiane, I had a drink with a U.S. Embassy official and learned that the United States was planning to build a new embassy in Laos. I wondered how much it would cost compared to the $5–10 million that the United States spends annually on the cleanup efforts. Upon returning from Laos, I checked the State Department website and found the estimated cost of the new embassy to be $110–145 million. The total of $50 million that the United States has spent to date on unexploded ordnance

1. See Rob Evans and David Leigh, "WikiLeaks Cables: Secret Deal Let Americans Sidestep Cluster Bomb Ban," *Guardian*, December 1, 2010, http://www.guardian.co.uk/world/2010/dec/01/wikileaks-cables-cluster-bombs-britain.

cleanup is also a small fraction of the hundreds of millions that have been spent looking for the bone fragments of pilots down in Laos and elsewhere in Indochina.

What most struck me on this visit to the Plain of Jars was the contrast between today's civilization on the Plain of Jars and the one described by the villagers in their essays.

The Plain has been declared a military zone by the Lao government, and thus, many living there today are soldiers and police officers—and their dependents—who have settled on the Plain since the war ended. Many of the newer villages stretch along either side of the main road so that they have access to electricity. Most of the farmland is still inaccessible to these subsistence-level farmers because of uncleared cluster bombs.

Therefore, the civilization described in these essays—of close-knit villages that had existed for centuries; villages where villagers prayed to their ancestors buried there, and expected to themselves be buried and revered one day; villages in which the highest joys derived from close relations with friends and relatives and within and between villages—no longer exists.

In September 1969, after a recorded history of seven hundred years, the Plain of Jars had disappeared.

Appendixes

Documentation on the air war in Laos may be secured from the U.S. Government Printing Office, Washington, DC; the documentation comprises two *Hearings before the Subcommittee to Investigate Problems Connected with Refugees and Escapees of the Committee on the Judiciary, United States Senate*, 92nd Cong. The first document is *War-Related Civilian Problems in Indochina, Part II: Laos and Cambodia* (April 21 and 22, 1971), from which we here (Appendix 1) reprint "Complete Text and Supporting Documents of USIS Refugee Survey as Obtained by Congressman McCloskey"; also in this hearing but not included here is "Documentation of American Bombing of Civilian Targets in Laos," prepared by Fred Branfman. The second document is entitled *World Refugee and Humanitarian Problems* (July 22, 1971), from which we here (Appendix 2) reprint excerpts of "A Survey of Civilian Casualties among Refugees from the Plain of Jars, Laos" by Walter M. Haney.

Appendix 1

Complete Text and Supporting Documents
of USIS Refugee Survey as Obtained by
Congressman McCloskey

FINDINGS OF AN OFFICIAL U.S.[1] SURVEY OF LAOS REFUGEES,
JULY 1970 (REFUGEES FROM XIENG KHOUANG PROVINCE)

In the past two weeks, our interviewers have talked with refugees from Xieng Khouang Province, located in twenty settlements, from the Phone Heng area in Thadeua District. Most of them came to the Vientiane plains with the group evacuated from the PDJ [Plaine des Jarres] in February of this year (1970). They came from 96 villages, located in 17 townships.

Bad weather and the usual travel impediments hampered the interviewers' movements and limited the scope of their findings. The lack of time and paucity of the interviewers' experience (only one of the four had ever been involved in such an exercise) were also limiting factors. Nevertheless, the relatively large number of people queried should give some degree of validity to the findings—at least enough to indicate general trends of thinking.

This group of people is atypical when compared to other refugees in Laos—the length of time they spent with the Pathet Lao separates them from the mass of refugees here. A separate report is being prepared on the people who have sought refuge from their homes in Saravane, Sam Neua and Luang Prabang. (People representing the latter two provinces now at Ban Na San—Site 272.) A cable will be prepared for the Ambassador on the 272 people.

Some findings:

1. For many of the questions, the number of responses is less than the total number of people interviewed; i.e., 150 may have answered one question, 180 another, etc. The primary reason for this is that I asked the interviewers not to carry the questionnaire with

1. Respondents' Background

96 percent of the respondents admitted to having lived under a Pathet Lao administered government, 63 percent of them from 1964 until they sought refuge with the RLG [Royal Lao Government] in 1969.

77 percent said their children are living with them; 20 percent indicated that their offspring are now with the Pathet Lao; and the remaining 3 percent told the interviewers their children are away from home serving in the FAR [Royal Lao Armed Forces].

Most of the people the interviewers talked with left their homes in 1969 (this was true of 93 percent). Including the move which took them to their current location, 48 percent said they had moved a total of three times since leaving their homes; 37 percent twice.

Nearly 50 percent said someone had arranged for their children to be taken to school—76 percent of this group said the PL [Pathet Lao] had provided this service. There was an exact correlation between the location of the schooling and the parents' reaction to it—if in the village, all concerned said it was desirable; if away from home, the people said they did not think it to be a good thing.

2. Aspects of Life under the PL

Finding what they liked and disliked about their experiences with the communists proved to be difficult—the refugees were quite naturally reluctant to speak with strangers about their feelings toward the communists. However, the interviewers did manage to get 210 responses (more than one response was allowed) to the question, "What did you like best about the PL?" Of this number, 22 percent saw "unity" as a positive aspect of their life with the PL. ("Unity" in this case means cooperative farming, communal

---

them while conducting the interview. They were instructed to wait until they could find a place away from the people interviewed to mark down the responses. This was done in an effort to keep the climate of the interview as relaxed and free form as possible. I also warned the interviewers about guessing when it came time to tabulate findings, thinking it better to skip the question than have a partially recalled answer marked down. The length of the questionnaire, the driving rains under which many of the interviews took place, and the generally inexact nature surrounding the whole process resulted in many blank answer sheets. However, the ratio of responses to number of respondents tabulated for each question should give us a reasonably accurate picture of the respondents' opinions.

arrangements for looking after children, etc.) 16 percent of the responses indicated "morality" (*sintham*) as a feature of life under the PL. (Note: No doubt one reason this was mentioned is the stealing of the refugees' cattle and water buffalo by the MR [Military Region] II troops prior to their evacuation from the PDJ). Nine percent said they liked the PL system of education.

Forced porterage was the least desirable aspect of life under the PL (41 percent of 363 responses). Next was taxation (36 percent). (Ref: McKeithen report provides a detailed account of life under the PL in Xieng Khouang.)

3. Bombing

97 percent of the people said they had seen a bombing attack—32 percent as early as 1964. 49 percent said they could not count the number of times they had seen bombs dropped, and 43 percent said they had seen planes bomb "frequently."

68 percent of 168 responses tabulated indicated that the respondents had seen someone injured by bombing, and 61 percent had seen a person killed. Given the period involved for most of the respondents (1964–1969) the number of people seen killed by bombing was extremely low—32 percent had seen only one person's death caused by a bomb. The only exception to this was one refugee from Mouang Soui who reported having seen 112 people killed during a bombing raid. (Unfortunately, the interviewer who talked with this man is now sick and had to be taken to a hospital in Bangkok, so it is impossible to get any more details about this case.) The other responses indicate a generally low casualty rate.[2]

This appears to be true for the enemy as well. Only 18 percent of the respondents said they had actually seen Lao-Viet troops killed by bombing, and 25 percent indicated they had heard rumors of deaths caused by bombing. The one outstanding exception reported was a T-28 strike on a

2. USAID refugee relief officer Edwin McKeithen reported one case involving refugees being killed by an air attack. It took place in June 1969, as villagers from Khang Khay were being led through the Site 119 valley to Nong Pet by PL sympathizers. The group of approximately 4,000 was caught in the open by four T-28s and fired upon repeatedly. The casualties, according to McKeithen, numbered over forty. After the attack, SGU [Special Guerrilla Unit] troops intercepted roughly 300 of the people and USAID moved them to site 240, in transit to Lat Saen. But before they could be moved, LS 240 fell and nearly half of the people were recaptured by the enemy, presumably to resume their march to Nong Het.

cave near Xieng Khouangville used by the PL as a communications center. The air attack was reported as having done away with the comma installation as well as some eighty PL troops who were in the cave at the time. Other cases reported in which relatively large numbers of enemy were killed by bombing, included 20 PL meeting their end at Phou Com Phet, 30 at Phou Kha Boh, and 20 at Phou Tuong.

That the bombing raised havoc with the lives of the people while they were in the PDJ area is not to be denied. 75 percent of 190 respondents said their homes had been damaged by bombing. 76 percent said the attacks took place in 1969. 99 percent of 212 respondents said the bombing made life difficult for them. 63 percent of this group told our interviewers that they were prevented from earning more than a bare subsistence living during the most intense periods of bombing. 37 percent reported building a shelter in the woods after they first saw a bombing raid.

Even after being exposed to such trials, 74 percent of the respondents said they understood the air attacks were caused by the PL waging war. But, 23 percent told the interviewers that the bombing is directed not only at the PL but also the people—13 percent said it was aimed at the people only. 71 percent of 238 responses indicated the U.S. is responsible for the bombing; only 17 percent laid the onus on the RLG. The 38 percent who had seen T-28s dropping bombs said they had seen jets doing the same thing. Their familiarity with planes was considerable; F-105s were noted in some conversations, as were "sky raiders" and P-4-hs (???). The PL propaganda machine has been reasonably effective, although it would seem to be aimed at a highly receptive audience.

4. Refugees' Future Aspirations

With regard to their aspirations for the future, the responses gathered by our interviews did not yield a very clear picture. 49 percent of the people whose answers were tabulated on this point (111 of 226) said that fear of bombing was the reason for their seeking refuge away from their homes. 29 percent listed dislike of the PL as the reason for leaving. 15 percent said the RLG coming in and either allowing or encouraging them to move was a primary factor in making them refugees.

The bombing is clearly the most compelling reason for moving. 57 percent of all 213 respondents said they would return to their villages if the air attacks were stopped. However, nearly 96 percent said they would not go back if the PL were still in control of their homes.

There are several possible reasons for this latter response. One might be that the people really cannot imagine having PL in the vicinity of their homes without resultant bombing. Another might be a fear of having alienated the PL by coming to the RLG side, thus leaving themselves open to retribution. But probably the most intense is a simple desire to be away from the war and from all the suffering and hardship it brings.

My personal impression is that it was a combination of three factors that moved most of the refugees. The destruction of their home villages by bombing certainly instilled the type of fear that would make a person want to move. However, 31 percent of the people had lived with bombing since 1964. Though it was not as intense as in 1969, it still represented a threat to their homes and lives. Being forced to serve as a porter irritated a high percentage of the people. On the other hand, while living under the RLG brings with it some mistreatment, it is nevertheless a way of life which generally does not impose many restrictions. In my opinion, it was all these factors, coupled with the opportunity offered by the RLG's sweep over the PDJ in late 1969, that brought the people to the Vientiane government's side.

5. Attachments[3]

1. Tabulated Responses to the Questionnaire.
2. Biographical Sketch of Thao Vilay, a refugee from Xieng Khouang who held some of the discussions upon which the above report is based.
3. Narrative accounts of interviews with refugees from MRII.
4. Memorandum of Conversation with a Chinese woman who sought refuge from Xieng Khouangville.

---

3. Only part of which have been released to the Subcommittee.

Appendix 2

A Survey of Civilian Casualties among
Refugees from the Plain of Jars, Laos

WALTER M. HANEY,
IVS volunteer, Laos, 1970–71

A. BACKGROUND TO THE SURVEY

During the summer of 1970, I helped organize a program for Lao students to work during their school vacation. The program was funded by USAID Laos and organized by International Voluntary Services, Inc., Laos (IVS) together with the Lao Ministry of Youth and Sports. During the program, I became involved with students who were teaching refugee children in four camps near Vientiane. The refugees in these villages were part of the reported 15,000 who were evacuated from the Plain of Jars in February 1970. From their involvement with these refugees, the students in the summer program learned a great deal about the refugees' lives prior to their evacuation from the Plain of Jars. As the students told me of their experiences with the refugees, I became increasingly disturbed about what they had learned about bombing on the Plain of Jars. As a result of what I had learned from the students, I was moved to write a letter to the U.S. Ambassador to Laos, Mr. McMurtrie Godley, protesting what had evidently been the bombing of innocent civilians [see section F below]. I also sent copies of this letter to my Senators in Washington, Senators Hart and Griffin from Michigan.

In November, Ambassador Godley invited me to discuss the matter with him personally. In our discussion on Nov. 23, Ambassador Godley received me most cordially and expressed his deep concern over the question of bombing of innocent villagers. He told me that American aircraft in Laos adhere to strict rules of engagement which proscribe the bombing of inhabited villages except under highly unusual circumstances. He acknowledged, however, that mistakes do occur and that innocent civilians have on occasion been subject to aerial bombardment. He maintained, however, that considering the number of aerial sorties over Laos, the number of errors resulting in the bombing of innocent villagers had been remarkably few. He suggested that while refugees may talk of the bombing in general terms, very few can actually give first hand accounts of the deaths of civilians by bombing.

As a result of my letters to Senators Hart and Griffin, I received copies of a letter from a Mr. David Abshire of the United States Department of State. In his letter, dated November 23, 1970, Mr. Abshire stated [see section G below for full text of letter]:

"American air support of the Royal Lao Government . . . is furnished under rules of operation designed specifically to protect civilians and to limit attacks to military targets. There is no question but that there have been civilian victims of bombing errors which were due to both mechanical and human causes, but a continuing effort goes on, even in the heat of battle, to keep such errors to a strict minimum. The rules do not permit attacks on non-military targets and places out-of-bounds all inhabited villages."

One of the students in the summer program had written:

"During the bombing, if the planes couldn't select a place to bomb, but they saw some animals or people they would simply drop the bombs on them. This was the primary reason why the refugees fled from the homes of their birth and came here. . . . The most important reason why the refugees had to come here from their villages must be the bombing."

Obviously, there was a conflict between what American officials, on one hand and students in the summer program on the other, had told me about the bombing.

In November, I visited a refugee camp north of Vientiane at Ban Ilay. There, I talked with the sub-district chief, Than Thit Thong, of the Ban Ilay refugee camp. He told me that the planes had bombed only when North Vietnamese soldiers shot at the planes. However, more than a dozen villagers in the same camp told me of how their homes had been destroyed by bombing when there were no soldiers in their village.

Again, there was a conflict between official and non-official accounts of the bombing. What had actually happened on the Plain of Jars? What was the nature of the bombing? Were there only a few mistaken bombings of innocent civilians or, was bombing of civilians heavy enough to have been a "primary cause" for their flight to this side?

B. Method of the Survey

The information which I had gleaned from the students working with the refugees had been subject to a number of possible sources of error. First, the students had not set out specifically to get information about the refugees' experiences on the Plain of Jars. Thusly, between their off-hand reception of the information from the refugees and their later retelling to me, there may have been omissions and distortions. Further, the information from the students was of a general nature with very little specific information. Ambassador Godley had suggested that refugees talk of the bombing largely in general terms, but that few have first-hand specific information about civilian deaths from bombing. Perhaps this had been the case with the refugees with whom the students worked.

So, I set out to make a survey to gain specific information about what had happened on the Plain of Jars. During my vacation from school, December 23, 1970 to January 4, 1971, I visited ten refugee camps on the Vientiane Plain. In order to give my survey greater objectivity, I asked not only about bombing victims, but more generally about any civilian casualties of war. When I went into a village, following the Lao custom, I did not initiate my inquiry immediately. Rather, I conversed very generally with the villagers for thirty minutes or an hour. Only then would I express interest in the question of civilian war victims. My questioning followed this pattern. First, I would inquire if any of the refugees had had any civilian relatives killed while they still lived on the Plain of Jars. Were any relatives shot and killed, or bombed and killed by either Pathet Lao (PL) forces or by Royal Lao government (RLG) forces?

I asked only about incidents in which immediate relatives of my interlocutors had been killed or wounded, on the theory that information about such specific incidents would be more reliable than non-specific descriptions of the situation in general.

If an individual had had a civilian relative killed, I asked the following questions:

What was the name of the narrator?
From what village and district was he?
What was the name of the victim and his relationship to the narrator?
When did he die?
Why did he die?
What was he doing when he died?

Often I would ask additional questions in order to clarify the details of the incident.

During an interview I took notes on what was said. After the interview I asked the interviewee if I might be able to take his picture. Invariably people were happy to have their pictures taken. Further, I also taped most interviews.[4]

In the interviews in section C, the abbreviations listed below have been used.

T. Tasseng or subdistrict of the interviewee.

B. Ban or village of the interviewee.

N. Name of the interviewee or narrator.

(Names listed in parentheses in this category are those of whoever may have given most of the information during the interview, if it was someone other than the relative of the victim.)

V. Relationship and name of the civilian victim.

D. Date of the incident.

O. Direct cause of death.

C. Circumstances of the incident.

T. Tape on which the interview was recorded.

Interviews usually involved extensive discussions and interplay between myself, the interviewee and other refugees. These interviews as transcribed in section C are greatly abbreviated from the actual conversations. They were written from my notes and the tapes of the interviews. In some cases, I do not have tapes of the interviews. In these instances I have transcribed the interviews from my notes alone.

Please see section D for my evaluation of the veracity of the information found in the interviews.

4. I made these tapes surreptitiously. I feared that if refugees knew that they were being taped they would have felt less free to express themselves. I may have been wrong because in all cases refugees knew that I was taking complete notes on what was said, yet most expressed themselves with apparent forthrightness. Nevertheless, refugees did not know that I was taping our conversations.

C. Text of Interviews

Section I. Ban Veun Kham—Tasseng Phan (Thao Ounkham Phimmavong)
241 families 1269 people.

VILLAGES

1. Ban Phan.
2. Ban Nasay.
3. Ban Pung.
4. Ban Phonsay.
5. Ban Vene.
6. Ban Khong Tai.
7. Ban Khong Neua.
8. Ban Nong.
9. Ban Tang.
10. Ban Ko.

1. T. Phan.
   B. Pung.
   N. Pho Xieng Onh
   V. Father Pho Titkhanta Mother Me Sao Douang another woman.
   D. '66/7 (2 young cousins)
   O. Large bomb, "fire bomb" from T-28.
   C. They were at home. This was before everyone had fled their homes. A big, big bomb set everything on fire. "Mother was burned up, Father was burned up. The children were burned up. Everything was burned up." There were no soldiers in the village. T-1A.
2. T. Phan.
   B. Pung.
   N. Sao Noi.
   V. Pho Louang Ti—father.
   D. '66/1.
   O. T-28 bombi.
   C. There were no soldiers around.
T. 1A.
3. T. Phan.
   B. Khong Neua.
   N. Pho Kang Poua.

V. Son who was 8 years old.

D. '69/6.

O. T-28 bombi.

C. Boy ran for a hole but the planes dropped the bombi before he reached the shelter. No soldiers in the village. There were some PL soldiers in the area but they were far away. "The planes just shot and bombed the village." T. 1A. Later told me about his older brother Ba Pa who was also killed by bombi from a T-28. He was old and deaf and didn't hear the planes coming. (untaped.)

4. T. Phan.

B. Pung.

N. Me Sao Chanta.

V. Husband 38 y., three children, Sao Bouavan 12 y.; Sao Bouathong 9 y.; Sao Tui 8 y.

D. '69 or '68, 9th month.

O. Jet, big bomb (one of Sao Chanta's surviving children suggested it was F 105, but mother said she only knew it was a jet).

C. Father and children had gone to work in rice field north of village. They hid in hole when the planes came, but planes dropped bombs near the hole. They were killed by bomb fragments. No relatives of Sao Chan Ta have been killed by PL or NVN. "There were no soldiers in our village when the planes bombed."

T. 1A.

5. a.:

T. Phan.

B. Vene.

N. Pho Xieng Ta.

V. Daughter who was 6 y. old.

D. '69/6.

O. T-28 bombi.

C. The girl and her brother were running for hole but they didn't make it in time. The boy was wounded in his right thigh. He almost died also. There were no soldiers in the village when the bombing occurred. Xieng To says that he has had no relatives killed by PL or VN.

T. 1A.

5. b.:

 V. Wife's younger brother Ba Chun 40y.

 D. 1965.

 O. Gunshot.

 C. He had gone to upland ricefield he was returning through the forest when some Meo soldiers shot him. They also shot three other villagers that day.

T. 1A.

6. a.:

 T. Phan.

 B. Tang.

 N. Xieng Boua Pha.

 V. Younger brother Thao La.

 D. '63/9.

 O. Mine.

 C. He had gone to fetch buffalo about 6 p.m. He stepped on a mine at the edge of village. The Meo soldiers had put the mine there.

T. 1A.

6. b.:

 V. Son of his younger brother.

 D. '67/1.

 O. Mine.

 C. The boy was a novice monk. He stepped on the mine at the edge of the wat at about 12 noon. The Meos put in all the mines. No relatives killed by PL or VN.

T. 1A.

6. c.:

 V. Daughter of older sister.

 D. '68/8 about 6 p.m.

 O. 155 mm shell.

 C. She was in Ban Ko near Muong Soui. There were RLG soldiers in the village. A 155 mm shell landed in the village and a shell fragment killed her in her home.

T. 1A.

7. T. Phan.

 B. Khong Neua.

N. Sao Deuang.

V. Younger brother Thao Ba La.

D. '64.

O. Gunshot.

C. He had gone to forest to look for food and things which he could sell. Region 2 Meo soldiers shot him. They shoot anyone they see in the forest.

T. 1B.

8. T. Phan.

B. Vene.

N. Tit Rhamsing.

V. Son Thao Sisouphan 8y.

D. '69/5.

O. Jet, big big bomb.

C. All of the family was in a hole together. The jet—maybe it was F105—dropped big bombs. Sisouphan was hurt inside. He ran around like he was drunk. He died 15 days later. There had been PL soldiers in the village. Didn't count how many but thought it was a company. They were staying—living and eating with the villagers. They left the hour before the jets came.

T. 1B.

9. T. Phan.

B. Khong Neua.

N. Sao Saphan.

V. Younger brother Xham Si 12y.

D. '64(?) "The year when the PL came to Xieng Khouang for the first time."

O. Gunshot.

C. He was walking in the forest going to upland ricefield. He was going there to raise food for us. The Meo soldiers shot and killed him. Shot him right through his cheek bones (When I asked if any other relatives had been killed by shooting or bombing they said,) No, but in Ban Khong Tai in 1970 just before we came here the bombing was very very heavy. All kinds of jets. We had to stay in the holes all the time. Even at night the planes shot and bombed. And they would drop flares. There were no soldiers in our village. In the month before we came to this side the bombing was heaviest.

Section II. Ban Phao—Tasseng Fat, 134 families, 768 people.

VILLAGES

1. Ban Fat Soi.
2. Ban Muong.
3. Ban Vieng.
4. Ban Nhat Si.
5. Ban Napheung.
6. Ban Khouane.

BAN PHAO INTERVIEWS

1. T. Fat.
   B. Napheung.
   N. Me Tum.
   V. Daughter Me Pao.
   D. '69/4.
   O. Jet bombi "F-4-hat".
   C. She was walking along path when jets dropped bombi. Tasseng said that there were PL and VN soldiers in the village when planes bombed.

   T. II A.

2. T Fat.
   B. Ban Nhat.
   N. Sao Leh.
   V. Son Xieng Thong Chan.
   D. '68/12.
   O. F105 bombi.
   C. We were already living in holes then because the planes always shot up the village. Thong Chanh had gone to the forest to find things to eat and there was no place for him to hide when the planes came. We lived in the holes for five years, but the bombing was only really heavy for two years '68–'69. We had to run to go cook or work in the ricefield. The planes came everyday T-28s, and F105s. But it was mostly F105s. The bombi came from a big bomb which exploded when it was still high in the air. The bombi were round and fell over a wide area. There were at least three hundred in each big cylinder. They exploded pom, pom, pom. It was impossible to

flee. When the little pieces hit a person they twisted and turned inside the body.

T. 2A.

3. T. Fat.
   B. Nhat.
   N. Sao Home.
   V. Son Xieng Boun Song 16 yrs.
   D. '68/12.
   O. Bombi from jet "F105".
   C. Had gone out to the forest to get things to eat. The planes came very fast and he couldn't find—place to hide in time. No relatives were shot or killed by the PL or VN.

T. 2A.

4. a.:
   T. Fat.
   B. Napheung.
   N. Bondi.
   V. Sisters Sao Nong 35y and cousin Xieng Boua Phan 26y.
   D. 68/12/17.
   O. Bombi from T-28.
   C. We were just starting to flee to this side, when the planes dropped the bombs on us. We had just come out of our holes. There were no PL NVN soldiers around. There were many people together but only these two were killed. There were no soldiers with us.

T. 2A.

4. b.:
   V. Father Xieng Boua Phan 62y, cousin Thao Kham.
   D. '69/10.
   O. Gunshot.
   C. We were fleeing to this side when the Vietnamese soldiers saw us. A group of 12 soldiers caught them and shot them. There were seven of us together but they only caught these two. It was very dangerous when we were coming to this side. If the planes saw us they would shoot us. If the Vietnamese saw us they would capture us.

T. 2A.

5. T. Fat.
   B. FatSoi.

N. Sao Phim.

V. Mother Sao Sa about 50y.

D. '67/6.

O. Big bomb from T-28.

C. She was in the ricefield but didn't flee because there were no soldiers and she didn't think the planes would shoot. No relatives killed by PL or Meo soldiers.

T. 2A.

6. a.:

T. Fat.

B. Fat Soi.

N. Chang Khamdi.

V. Older brother Kang Chouk.

D. '66/1.

O. T-28 firebomb.

C. He was at home and the plane dropped a big firebomb, the house burned up. Everything burned up. There were no soldiers in the village.

T. 2A.

7. T. Fat.

B. Sang.

N. Me Sanout.

V. Son Titsomphan 23 y.

D. '67/3.

O. Bullets from a T-28.

C. He was coming back from the market when the planes came. He didn't flee in time. Three or four PL soldiers were also killed at the same time.

T. 2A.

8. a.:

T. Fat.

B. Nhat.

N. Sao Som.

V. Younger brother Bathon 28 y.

D. '66/6.

O. Bullets from a T-28.

C. He had gone to visit relatives. He was sitting in the house just like
we are now. The planes shot the house and he died immediately.
There were no soldiers in the village.

T. 2A.

8. b.:

B. Leng.

N. Sao Som.

V. Son Douangsi 22 y.

D. '66/7/13.

O. Gunshot.

C. He was sleeping in wat when the Vietnamese came and shot up the
wat. They wanted to get the monks' belongings.

T. 2A.

8. c.:

T. Kheung.

B. Ban Ang.

N. Sao Som.

V. Relative, in-law Xieng Nohn 47 y.

D. '67/11.

O. Gunshot.

C. He was at home in RLG controlled area. The Vietnamese shot
up the house at night. They wanted money. His wife and child
died also.

[There are a total of 189 interviews describing deaths. Of special interest
are several that talk of the "poisons dropped by the planes," which follow
herewith.]

T. 6A.

12. T. Xieng.

B.

N. Thanh Boun Song (Tasseng Xieng Secretary) and group of 5–6
other villagers (I asked if the airplanes had ever dropped poison on
their villages) Yes, they dropped it on us. It was the F105 jets which
dropped it. It was long. It looked like the little noodles from
Chinese soup. The Vietnamese said that it was poison. The Pathet
Lao taught us to get long sticks and use the sticks to move it into

holes and bury it. Also there was another kind of poison which looked like salt. After buffalo ate grass on which it was dropped they died. The paper kind sometimes was in very long pieces two or three meters. It looked like thin strips of paper. Like if you cut a piece of white paper into small strips. We were afraid to touch it.

T. (No tape.)

13. (I returned to Van Pheung on Jan 2 because I had not recorded the villagers' description of the poison on Jan 1. See #12).

T. Xieng.

N. Thanh Boun Song (Tasseng Xieng Secretary).

Yes, there are many kinds of things which the villagers called poison, but it's not important. We don't really know where it came from. Whether it came from the planes or whether someone brought it, we're not sure. No, I never saw any poison. In Xieng Khouang all I saw was the bombs that exploded sending out many small white particles. If the chickens ate it they would die. It was small and white like salt.

(At this point other villagers, including village chief of Ban Kang Pa. Xieng Pheng joined in the conversation.) No, it wasn't like paper. You see there were two kinds, one like salt and the other like paper. During the May and June of 1969 before the government (RLG) came, the bombing was the heaviest, they dropped many bombi. Both T-28's and jets dropped the bombi. Four villagers from Kang Pa died from the bombing in 1969. The bombing was the heaviest in May and June before the government (RLG) came in July. Yes, there were soldiers in the village when the planes dropped the bombs. Four or five Vietnamese always stayed with us. They were afraid that we would come to this side. If we moved from one place to another they would always move with us. There were more than 100 villagers in Kang Pa. Can't count how many times the planes dropped the bombi. No, we never saw any poison. Whether they dropped any poison in Kang Pa or not, I don't know. There were some people who got sick and drunk though. No, we never saw any poison. Never. (At this point one man in the background said that the planes sometimes dropped paper.) It was paper like this. In very small strips. (One man took the foil from a cigarette package and sent a small girl to get some scissors. When she brought them he started cutting the foil into small strips perhaps 2–4 mm wide.) The paper was like this. Both T-28's and jets dropped it. The Vietnamese told us that it was poison and that we shouldn't touch it or pick it up. Or sometimes they called it *ya mao* (literally "drunk medicine"). Or they said like in Vietnam K-nee poison. Animals never ate this kind of poison. They only ate the white kind which was like salt. The paper kind came in long long pieces. Sometimes three or four meters. They told us "this is poison. Don't touch it or you will get drunk and die." Even if you only touch it. We had to take sticks and bury it, we couldn't touch it. If we touched it, it would burn. It was like this (gesturing to the cut strands from the cigarette package foil) except much longer. The other kind was white, like salt. If buffalo ate it they would die. If it fell on grass all the grass would die. It came from the planes like the other kind. (There followed a general discussion of villagers killed by bombing, artillery and one woman killed by the "enemy" when she tried to come to this side. I didn't have time to get all of the details or even names.)

D. Evaluation of the Survey

Accuracy of the Interviews

When I first went into a village, I found that people sometimes were hesitant to talk to me about civilian war casualties. Particularly, I found that officials were hesitant to talk about such casualties. This hesitation seemed to vary directly with the level of the official. In November, I had found that many individual refugees in Ban Ilay had contradicted the account of the sub-district chief of that refugee camp who had told me that planes only bombed when Vietnamese soldiers shot at the planes first. On many occasions during my ten day survey, I again noticed contradictions in the accounts of minor officials and those of refugees holding no official positions. In the Veun Khene refugee camp, the sub-district chief showed me a list of civilian fatalities. I asked him why the people had died. He replied, "On account of the Pathet Lao."

I inquired further, "What do you mean? Were these people all shot by the Pathet Lao."

"No."

"I do not understand. What do you mean? Why did you say that the deaths of these people were caused by the Pathet Lao?"

He answered, "The people were killed by many things. But if the Pathet Lao had not been there, the people would not have been killed. And it was the fault of the Pathet Lao because they would not let the people come to this side. If those people could have come to this side they would not have been killed."

The logic of this sub-district chief is undeniable but Veun Khene refugees holding no official positions were much more explicit about the primary causes of individual war victims (see Interviews Section III).

Also, in the refugee camp in Dongkaloum the sub-district chief seemed to give a story quite different than that of most non-official refugees. In this village, the sub-district chief seemed to try to dissuade me from my inquiry. He told me, "There were very few civilian deaths. It's hard to say why they died. It was very confused, you know. On account of the war. You can't really get much information here, why don't you go look at the lists which we sent to Vientiane." The responses of individual refugees (see Dongkaleum Interviews Section VIII) again were much more explicit about causes of death.

I think, however, that most non-official refugees told me their stories with as much truth as their memories would serve them. Certain characteristics of our conversations indicated truthfulness. Conversations were not dominated by a single individual. Answers about details often came only after discussions among family or neighbors. Also, I found that after I had been in a village for a length of time, people volunteered information about which I would never have thought to ask; for instance, "poison." Nor was I particularly interested in people who had died from disease, except that in Nong Vang Pheung, women kept coming up to me wanting to relate how their children had died. Thus, I think that the interviews in section C are truthful insofar as the knowledge and the memories of the refugee interviewees would serve them.

This is not, however, to say that either the refugees' memories of, or even, original knowledge of particular incidents were completely faultless. More particularly I would judge the accuracy of the responses as follows. I feel that refugees knew their own sub-district, their village, their name, and that of their deceased relative, with complete accuracy. Also, I feel that people knew with accuracy the general cause of their relations' deaths such as bombing, mines, or small arms. When it came to identifying the specific cause, I would be less certain of reliability. For instance, people seemed to be able to tell the difference between what types of planes had been present, whether jets or propellor driven planes, but I would question identification of specific types of jets or propellor driven planes. One man told me quite simply that, "All the planes which went r-r-r-r-r-r-r and had propellors we called T-28's and all the kind which went rrrrrrrrrr and didn't have any propellors we called *ai phone* (jet) or *ef loi ha* (F 105)." However, it seems clear that more than just these two types of aircraft took part in the bombing. Many people told me about a second type of jet which they called *ef si hat* (F 4-H). also, types of propellor driven craft other than T-28's were identified. A further difficulty in the identification of the aircraft responsible for an individual's death was that, sometimes, different types of aircraft were reported to have been present together. People simply didn't know with much accuracy, in such cases, which planes had dropped which bombs or caused which deaths.

Almost invariably refugees reported that RLG forces were the source of mines and artillery fire which killed villagers. Such opinions seem to be based entirely on the fact that the people were living in PL controlled areas. The people have therefore assumed that any shelling or mining of the area must have been done by RLG forces. They seem to have no basis for such conclusions other than this assumption.

Another section of the interviews which ought to be judged with some reservation is that of the date of the incidents. Most of the refugees in the survey simply could not recall the day of the month on which a relative died. But, the particular month of the incidents, they seemed to know reliably.[5] The year of the incident was often a source of much discussion. In a number of cases people told me that relatives died on the Plain of Jars in the summer of 1970. This was completely impossible since the refugees had come to Vientiane in February of 1970. When I asked if they were sure it was 1970 or "But when did you come to Vientiane," they would simply reply, "Oh, then it must have been 1969." So I would suggest that the years given for the incidents are not always completely accurate.

5. Refugees could recall the months of particular incidents reliably because they could relate incidents to seasonal activities such as planting rice in the sixth or seventh month or harvesting rice in the eleventh or twelfth month. The Lao calendar is one month ahead of the Western calendar (i.e. the seventh month Western calendar is the eighth month Lao calendar) so that if a narrator did not specify by which calendar he was reckoning, I would ask, "Do you mean Lao calendar or Western (*sao kone*)?"

Beyond these reservations, I believe that the information in these interviews is quite accurate.

Summary

1. General Pattern of the Bombing

From 1964 to 1969, villagers on the Plain of Jars were subjected to dangers from many sources. It is clear, however, that the major source of hazard for these people was aerial bombardment (see Tables 1 and 2). The bombing was particularly heavy in 1968 and 1969. This bombing was done by a variety of jet and propeller driven aircraft, using a wide variety of ordnance. Among the ordnance dropped by the planes, the following were described to me by refugees from the Plain of Jars:

a. "big, big bombs" or "500kg" bombs.

b. smaller or "regular" bombs which apparently were in the 150–250kg class.

c. Anti-personnel bombs or what the refugees called "bombi." These were evidently of two different types. The most commonly described type was round, roughly 8–10cm in diameter. The other, less frequently described variety, was larger and rested on a set of "legs." See pictures number 1 and 2 which contain drawings by refugees of these two types to anti-personnel weapons. Picture number 3 shows pellets which reportedly came from one of the "bombi." Refugees had gathered these pellets to use in their home-made muskets.

d. Napalm referred to by refugees as *bom napan* or *bom fai* (fire bomb).

The 74 incidents of aerial bombardment involving 108 casualties were described to me as follows:

	Number of incidents	Number of casualties
I. No PL or NVN soldiers present at time of incident	58	91
II. PL soldiers present at time of incident	5	6
III. Presence or absence of soldiers not noted in the interview	11	11

In two of the incidents in the first category it was reported that Pathet Lao soldiers had been present in the village but had left just before the bombing.

One of the incidents in the second category, involving two deaths, was that of the prison bombing described in the next section.

2. Bombing of Pathet Lao Prison

While I was interviewing refugees in the Dongkaleum refugee camp, three individuals independently described to me the bombing of a Pathet Lao prison in 1968. The first time I heard of the incident, the description was very vague. The man told me only that sixty prisoners of the "Lao Issara" (Pathet Lao) had been killed when the planes bombed a prison in the forest near Ban Sang. The other two descriptions were much more explicit. (See Dongkaleum Interviews No. VIII 13 and VIII 16.) Both of these refugees told me that the bombing of the jungle prison occurred on July 5, 1968. Of the more than 100 prisoners in the jail, sixty-three died. The prison was reportedly bombed by T-28s and jets. Ironically, these prisoners were evidently political (i.e. anti-Pathet Lao). These stories were corroborated in an informal conversation which I had with a refugee from the Ban Ilay refugee camp. However, this individual said that of the sixty-three fatalities from the prison bombing, sixty were prisoners and three were Pathet Lao guards.

3. "Poison" Dropped by Aircraft

As I mentioned earlier, I stumbled on to an account of civilian deaths due to "poison" quite by accident. When I first heard the account of the childrens' deaths due to "poison" I did not quite believe it. I thought that the refugees were simply using the word "poison" to describe napalm which had not ignited. Only after I had returned to get details of the "poison" did I really comprehend that they were describing something quite distinct from napalm (see Nakung Interviews VI 9 and 12). After this first story about the poison, I began to make gentle inquiries about it in other refugee camps. Altogether, I heard first hand accounts of the poison in three camps, of the last four camps which I visited; Nong Vang Pheung, Nakung and Thoun Loua. Refugees in the Ban Mak Nao camp had never seen any of the "poison". I had visited all of the other refugee camps prior to first hearing about the "poison" and so had made no inquiries about it in the majority of the villages which I visited.

Two types of "poison" were described to me.

    a. The most commonly described type of "poison" (Mong Vang Pheung, Nakung, and Thoun Loua) looked like paper. In two cases (Nakung and Nong Vang Pheung) refugees described it as being long strips of silver colored paper. Some refugees compared it to the small thin noodles in Chinese soup. One man compared it to rice straw. One man said that it was the color of my silver watch and others said that it was the color of the foil paper from a cigarette package. Evidently this paper was dropped in long tangled masses. According to the refugees it killed both plants and animals. A paper sort of "poison" was also described to me in the Thou Loua camp but here the refugees described it as sheets rather than strips. Further, I have received reports that the refugees in the Veun Kham camp and the Ban Ilay camp both talk about this paper "poison." In both cases the refugees reportedly describe it as looking like long strips of silver colored paper.

This type of "poison" sounds suspiciously like radar chaff which might have been dropped by the airplanes in order to jam radar controlled antiaircraft installations in the area. For obvious political reasons the Pathet Lao might have identified such radar chaff as poison. I suggested this explanation to one refugee. He replied that, yes, the planes sometimes did drop the "radar paper". He said that the poison paper looked almost exactly like the radar paper but could be distinguished from it in four ways;

i. If the paper poison was touched it would feel hot or at least warm.

ii. If the paper poison was immersed in water it would bubble. (Reportedly making the water toxic.)

iii. If the paper poison was hit or moved roughly it would give off a fine dust.

iv. The poison paper was toxic to both plants and animals. These distinctions between the "poison paper" and radar chaff are rather tenuous and at any rate were probably unknown to the majority of the refugees. Therefore, I think it safe to assume that at least some of the reports of the poison silver paper were merely reports of radar chaff.

b. The second type of "poison" described to me was of a granular or powdery character. I have personally received accounts of it only from refugees in the Nong Vang Pheung camp. There, refugees compared it to salt. They said that any fruit trees or grass on which it was dropped would die. Also they said that it was toxic to many kinds of animals which would forage in an area where it was dropped.

Also in an interview taped by a Lao friend of mine, refugees in Ban Veun Kham told of this type of poison. They described it as looking like yellow flour. They compared the color to the yellow of a khaki uniform. They reported that on one occasion it was dropped on a field and after grazing there thirty cows died. They said that if pigs or chickens foraged in an area where it had been dropped they would die with their flesh turning yellow and intestines green. They said further that it would kill plants as well.

4. Other Devices

A wide variety of other explosive and poisonous devices have been described to me. However, such reports are usually second or third hand. Or, if first hand, have been reported by only a single individual. I therefore will omit any discussion of these devices. I can only hope that these reports are the products of Pathet Lao propaganda and have no basis in fact.

5. Porterage

Of the incidents described in this survey, eleven involve the deaths of civilians either while portering for the Pathet Lao (eight) or while returning from porterage duties (three.) Of these eleven individuals, eight were reported killed by mines and one each by artillery, aerial bombardment and small arms. Four were reported killed prior to 1966, three in 1966–67, three in 1968–69 and in one case the year was not noted.

It is interesting to note how the refugees referred to porterage. Six said simply that the victims had gone portering *(pai lam liang)*. Others reported that the victims had been ordered *(bang khap)*, *forced (inum)*, caught *(chap)*, or organized *(chat)*, into portering.

While I did not delve into the question of porterage extensively these descriptions indicate that coercion was often involved in the organization of porterage.

6. Presence of North Vietnamese Soldiers.

Again, this is a question into which I did not delve directly. However, the mention of Vietnamese soldiers *(thahaan keo,* or *thahaan Vietnam;* and I think it safe to assume that refugees were referring to North rather than South Vietnamese) in six separate interviews indicates that North Vietnamese soldiers certainly were present on the Plain of Jars. Two refugees simply mentioned the presence of Vietnamese soldiers (Interviews III and X 6). Two related that Vietnamese soldiers shot villagers as they were trying to flee to this side (Interviews II 4b and IV 3a). One narration by a group of refugees in Ban Wong Vang Pheung (Interview IX 13) told of how Vietnamese had lived with the villagers in order to prevent them from coming to RLG controlled territory. And one refugee (Interview II 8) related that Vietnamese soldiers had killed villagers in order to get their belongings.

E. Conclusion

This survey was by no means a complete survey of all of the civilian war casualties among refugees from the Plain of Jars. Nor was it a complete survey of all of the civilian war casualties from any of the refugee villages which I visited. Rather it was *a random sampling comprised of all those case histories of civilian war victims which I could gather in the time available to me. The villages which I visited contain approximately 8500 of the 25,000 refugees from the Plain of Jars now residing on the Vientiane Plain.*

If the sampling in this survey is representative of the experience of the refugees from the Plain of Jars as a whole, then *the following conclusions may be drawn;*

1. *Aerial bombardment was the primary cause of civilian war casualties among refugees from the Plain of Jars while under Pathet Lao control 1964–1969.*

2. *Contrary to the policy statements of American officials, bombardment of the civilian population of the Plain of Jars by aircraft, including large numbers of American jets, was extensive and caused large numbers of civilian casualties.*

F. Letter to G. McMurtie Godley, U.S. Ambassador to Laos

Dear Mr. Ambassador: During the summer of 1970, I helped organize a program for Lao students to work during their school vacation. The program was funded by USAID and organized by International Voluntary Services, Inc., Laos, working together with the Lao Ministry of Youth and Sports.

During the program I became especially involved with students who were teaching children in four refugee villages near Vientiane. These refugees were part of the reported 15,000 who were evacuated from the Plain of Jars in February 1970. The students in the program taught in the refugee villages for lengths of time varying from four weeks to ten weeks. The variations in program length were necessitated by our limited budget. The program was moderately successful, but that is not what concerns me here. Rather, I would like to relate some of the profoundly disturbing stories of the refugees' lives prior to their evacuation from the Plain of Jars as told to students in the summer program. I shall omit students' names since they were fearful of personal repercussions.

Ban Ilay

Refugees in Ban Ilay told students of how their houses were burned in 1963 by gunfire from the Pathet Lao. The people were then relocated by the Pathet Lao. Jets started bombing their village in 1964, and bombed most heavily in 1966. The refugees had to live in holes in the ground. At first they tried cultivating rice at night. But then the planes started bombing at night. If the villagers started even a small fire, they would be bombed and strafed by the planes. Villagers said that they had to live in holes in the ground for three years.

Dan Na Nga

The approximately 2000 refugees in this village came from Ban Lat Sene in Xieng Khouang province. They said that the bombing started there in 1967. The bombing was so heavy in the daytime that villagers could work in their ricefields only at night. All of the people's homes were destroyed so they had to live in the forest or in caves in the mountains. In 1969 the planes started dropping flares at night and bombing by the light of the flares.

At first the villagers simply fled when they heard the sound of a plane. But then the PL taught them how to use rifles to shoot at the planes. Some of the children (again according to the refugees as told to the students in the summer work program) became very adept at shooting down the planes. When the refugees came down from the Plain in February 1970, one or two of the young men and women from each family stayed with the Pathet Lao. I asked one of the students why these young people had stayed with the P.L. He replied, "Because the P.L. lied to them and persuaded them to stay. The young people chose to stay with the P.L., but it was because the outlaws (P.L.) lied to them."

I then asked this same student why he thought these villagers had been bombed by the airplanes. He answered, "Because there were Pathet Lao soldiers in the village."

I enquired further, "Do you mean that Pathet Lao had a camp in the village?"

"No, but some of the boys in the village had joined the Pathet Lao, and they were living and working with their families."

Many of the refugees told students that they do not like life in Ban Na Nga. They went there on account of the bombing; and when the bombing stops, they want to go back to their homes.

Ban Nongsa

Villagers in Ban Nongsa related to students working there that they had not liked living with the Pathet Lao because the Pathet Lao had not allowed them to practice their Buddhist beliefs. If the people gave offerings to the monks, they would be ridiculed by the Pathet Lao. The P.L. would ask them where they got the offerings to waste on the monks.

They would suggest that perhaps the offerings came from the government (RLG) side where many people still follow such wasteful traditions.

Refugees told how they had to farm at night because if they worked in the ricefields during the daytime the planes would shoot at them. Also it was impossible to show any kind of a light at night because the planes would see it and shoot at it. Villagers told how they had to live in holes in the ground or in the forest for two or three years.

Ban Veun Kham

Refugees in this village told students how they had to live in holes in the ground for three years. The planes would shoot or bomb any people whom they saw. Sometimes the planes would even bomb cattle or buffalo. Villagers even told how once some monks in their orange robes had been strafed by a jet as they came out of their cave. One man told how his wife had gone out to fetch their water buffalo and had been strafed by a jet.

The above information comes from the refugees as told to students in the summer work program. The appended article comes from the same source. None of this is information which has been dug out by a reporter or by anyone else with a particular viewpoint to push. It is information which students in the summer program discovered through their work in the refugee villages. Some of the students were quite agitated about what they learned from the refugees. Previous to their summer work experience, they had thought that such stories were merely Pathet Lao propaganda. Some of them now think quite differently.

Undoubtedly, some of the stories were related to me with imperfect accuracy. And after working in Laos for more than two years, I would readily admit that some of the stories may have been embellished by the villagers in their original telling. But out of these stories from four separate villages, one fact seems to emerge incontrovertibly. The United States has been waging an extensive bombing campaign against the civilian populations of portions of Pathet Lao occupied territory.

Exactly what portion of the bombing has been conducted by US aircraft and what portion by Royal Lao aircraft is unclear. But this distinction is a spurious one. Whether the bombs were dropped by US planes or by RLG planes is immaterial. Even if all of the bombs were dropped by RLG aircraft the United States is culpable, simply because we train and supply the Royal Lao Air Force.

Surely, evils have been perpetrated by the Pathet Lao. Refugees' stories testify to this. As the student author of the appended article has written. "Wickedness was always with the people . . . Lawlessness was present on both sides."

But a large part of the "lawlessness" perpetrated on these "Laotions who had done no evil but still reaped such misfortune," seems directly attributable to policies of the United States government.

As an American I feel compelled to protest these policies. The bombing of innocent civilian population is, to me, completely inexcusable.

Sincerely yours,
Walter M. Haney.

G. Letter to Senator Robert P. Griffin

Dear Senator Griffin: I have received your communication transmitting the letter of Mr. Walter Haney of Vientiane concerning the grave effects of the war in Laos on the civilian population of the country.

The President on March 6 made public the fact that we provide air support for the neutral government of Laos, which is defending itself against invasion by more than 60,000 troops of North Viet-Nam. North Viet-Nam, like us, signed the Geneva Agreements of 1962, which specifically forbid the introduction of foreign troops into Laos. Despite this, the North Vietnamese continue to use Lao territory in the southern part of the country for a large road network serving their war aims in South Viet-Nam, and in North Laos have expelled the neutral Royal Lao Government of Souvanna Phouma from a large part of the national territory, particularly those areas of Laos near North Viet-Nam.

American air support of the Royal Lao Government, which is directed against North Vietnamese troop concentrations, lines of communication and logistic stores, is furnished under rules of operation designed specifically to protect civilians and to limit attacks to military targets. There is no question but that there have been civilian victims of bombing errors which were due to both mechanical and human causes, but a continuing effort goes on, even in the heat of battle, to keep such errors to a strict minimum. The rules do not permit attacks on non-military targets and place out-of-bounds all inhabited villages. In cases where it is believed there may be a question about the nature of the target, a Lao national is required to participate in the control bombing operations. The rules of operation are the subject of continual review.

In contrast to the North Vietnamese/Pathet Lao, we also give major support to the Lao Government to relocate members of the civilian population who freely choose to move away from the areas of fighting, and to provide them with food and medical care.

The reports of the refugees which Mr. Haney has received through the Lao students who worked with him last summer attest vividly to the suffering which the war has imposed on the Lao, perhaps most harshly of all in the northeastern part of the country from which these refugees come. It is clear that danger comes to the civilian population from both of the combatant sides, and also that the line between civilian and soldier is blurred, as the passage on villagers' efforts to shoot down aircraft illustrates.

Mr. Haney attributes a large part of the misfortune inflicted on the villages to the policies of the United States government. These policies, however, are undertaken not independently but at the request of the Royal Lao Government, acting in response to the unprovoked invasion of that neutral country by North Viet-Nam.

Like the Royal Lao Government, our Government has repeatedly protested North Viet-Nam's imposition of war on Laos, which seeks no more than neutrality and to be left alone. We deeply regret the fate of all the victims of the war, both those killed by North Vietnamese action, and those whose lives have been lost or disrupted as a consequence of the defense of their country.

If we can be of further assistance on this or any other matter, please do not hesitate to let us know.

SINCERELY YOURS,
DAVID M. ABSHIRE,
Assistant Secretary for
Congressional Relations.